Coach Mac has taken a courageous stance in engaging the Messianic Jewish community. I am blessed to be a member of this community. The coach's challenge is for the church to open her arms widely and accept us as equal partners in the kingdom. Coach Mac's approach to biblical reconciliation is a fresh perspective. I wholeheartedly endorse the book!

RABBI ROBERT COHEN, Congregation Beth Jacob

■　■　■　■　■

Coach Mac has given a wonderful gift to pastors and leaders in Christ. Thank you, Bill, for speaking the truth in love in this life-changing, revolutionary book!

CHE AHN, CEO and chairman of The Call

■　■　■　■　■

Bill McCartney is a prophetic voice in our time! *Blind Spots* is a clear, courageous, compelling call not only to deal with the blind spots that plague the body of Christ but also to fully embrace God's vision for who and what he has called us to be. The message of this book will challenge your thinking and change your life.

DR. CRAWFORD W. LORITTS, JR., author, speaker, radio host, and associate director of Campus Crusade for Christ, USA

■　■　■　■　■

This new book by Coach puts us in touch with a great heart. Coach Mac puts forth a vision and practical direction for moving toward the fullness of the church. Here is a vision for unity, righteousness, power, reconciliation, witness, Jewish rootedness, and much more. It is the right vision and direction for these days in which we live.

DANIEL JUSTER, director of Tikkun International, a Messianic Jewish Ministry

■ ■ ■ ■ ■

More than any man I know, Coach McCartney has a passionate heart for God and the church. Read this book and the fire in Mac's heart just might be transferred to you!

DR. ERWIN W. LUTZER, senior pastor of The Moody Church

■ ■ ■ ■ ■

I've known Coach Mac for twenty-five years. With joy I have watched his faith and obedience grow from spiritual infancy to deep maturity. This is clearly the most important book he has yet written for the church in North America. I heartily encourage an aggressive, prayerful reading of this important and much needed book! It could be the divine spark that the church needs to build a fire of true awakening.

DR. JOHN H. ARMSTRONG, president of Reformation & Revival Ministries

■ ■ ■ ■ ■

Like the man who wrote it, this book is passionate, compelling, and straight to the heart! Coach is one of the greatest men I've ever known. He's more than a coach. He's an inspiration, a mentor, and a friend. He and this great work are a beacon of light that America needs to follow!

JOE WHITE, president of Kanakuk Kamps

■ ■ ■ ■ ■

Just as there is a blindness covering the eyes of the Jewish people today that keeps them from recognizing Jesus (Yeshua) as their Messiah, there is a blindness covering the eyes of Christians that keeps them from recognizing God's plan for Israel and the Jewish people in these last days. God has opened Coach Mac's eyes to this and is using him to strip away this blindness from the church. *Blind Spots* is a wake-up call to us all.

RABBI JONATHAN BERNIS, Jewish Voice Ministries International

■　■　■　■　■

Don't let this book get caught in your "blind spot." . . . It is a must-read for all of us involved in ministry to keep ourselves focused on the ultimate goal of honoring God in all of our relationships.

DR. JOSEPH M. STOWELL, president of Moody Bible Institute

■　■　■　■　■

I believe *Blind Spots* is long overdue! I highly recommend that every person in the body of Christ read it. Coach addresses a very important topic that is relevant to the kingdom of God. His straightforward approach to one of the weightier issues confronting the church will, no doubt, play a key role in facilitating change throughout the body of Christ. No one can accuse this man of God of having an underlying agenda, because there is none. Maybe one and that is, "THE WILL OF GOD!"

BISHOP LARRY JACKSON, senior pastor of Bethel Outreach International Church

■　■　■　■　■

I believe that two things are important to God: (1) motivation and (2) what results you want to achieve. I think John 17 is the right motivation—Jesus' High Priestly prayer. Reconciliation is the ministry of the church. I believe that the book *Blind Spots* addresses those two issues, and I think Coach is the person to keep pounding until the church becomes a praise in the earth and the world can see a model of heaven on earth (Matthew 6:10).

BISHOP WELLINGTON BOONE, senior pastor of The Father's House

■　■　■　■　■

Bill McCartney is an instrument of the Holy Spirit who is seeking to anoint our eyes with eye salve, that we may see! (Revelation 3:18).

JACK HAYFORD, pastor of The Church on the Way

■　■　■　■　■

As you read through this book, you will come to realize that all of us have blind spots. The question is, are you ready to acknowledge them and do something about them? A blind spot has a way of turning into a "sore spot" that can fester unless dealt with. America needs healing, and it must start with me. A must-read for all pastors!

REV. DANIEL DE LEON, senior pastor of Templo Calvario and member of Promise Keepers Board of Directors

■　■　■　■　■

My dictionary tells me that [the etymology of] *transparent* from its Latin roots means "to show oneself." Coach McCartney['s model] has always embodied this word. Whether in private conversations or public preaching, he demonstrates Paul's exhortation to the Ephesians: "But the light makes all things easy to see, and everything that is made easy to see can become light" (Ephesians 5:13, *New Century Version*). It is his sincere willingness to share how God made "dark" areas light that enables us to "see" the blind spots that have often crippled many of us. I heartily recommend this book as a basic manual for humility and growth.

BISHOP JOSEPH L. GARLINGTON, SR., Ph.D., senior pastor of Covenant Church of Pittsburgh and president of Reconciliation! Ministries International

　　　＊　＊　＊　＊　＊

The mark of every significant book is the impact it makes on the reader. It is a given that books worth reading present helpful material. But significant books also impact the heart of the reader. Coach Mac's *Blind Spots* does this. This book grips the soul of men on issues too easily ignored. I can hear Coach encouraging all of us men and pastors on each page. His energetic spirit encourages me to face needed adjustments in my own life, step out in faith with those adjustments, and then pick up the tools of ministry to help men around me do the same.

Coach Mac presents a forthright word on a specific issue that faces men today: unity no matter what other men may look like. He paints an accurate picture of the divided church and addresses in detail a way to solve the problem. Differences of ethnicity and culture can be overcome in Christ. Coach blends a practical approach, showing how men can *relate* to one another.

In a boldly frank discussion on unity in the Body of Christ, he gives practical reasons to get back into ministry as it touches the heart of God. Coach gives us a game plan to tackle challenges of intimacy to all in the family of God. It is a must-read for men, especially pastors who long to see their men live boldly for Christ.

BRUCE W. FONG, Ph.D., president of Michigan Theological Seminary and member of Promise Keepers Board of Directors

WHAT

YOU

DON'T

SEE

MAY BE

KEEPING

YOUR

CHURCH

FROM

GREATNESS

blind

BILL McCARTNEY

spots

Tyndale House Publishers, Inc., Wheaton, Illinois

Visit Tyndale's exciting Web site at www.tyndale.com

Blind Spots

Designed by Dean H. Renninger

Edited by Curtis H. C. Lundgren

Library of Congress Cataloging-in-Publication Data

McCartney, Bill, date.
   Blind spots : what you don't see may be keeping your church from greatness / Bill McCartney.
      p. cm.
Includes bibliographical references (p.   ).
   ISBN 0-8423-6998-8 (hc);   ISBN 0-8423-8450-2 (custom sc)

   1. Christian men—Religious life. 2. Church work with men—United States. 3. Race relations—Religious aspects—Christianity. 4. Promise Keepers (Organization) I. Title.

BV4440 .M295 2003
248.8'42—dc21   2002152705

Printed in the United States of America

08   07   06   05   04   03
7   6   5   4   3   2   1

When I considered to whom, other than my Lord and Savior Jesus Christ, I should dedicate this book, it didn't take long to receive the unbridled revelation as to whom that should be. Who helped me discover and address my greatest blind spot, the one that was the most destructive? Who stood with me for more than thirty years as I remained ignorant to the presence of this blind spot? Who loved me unconditionally in spite of the fact that she was the primary target of the destructive impact of this blind spot? Who is the one who even today loves me more than I love her, even though I love her with all my heart? Who, but my precious Lyndi!

contents

■　■　■　■　■

foreword

■ ■ ■ ■ ■

Ever been sovereignly set up by God?

Secretly set up to learn a profound truth or to experience life in such a way that it would forever cast its influence over your life?

Just moments ago, it dawned on me that the Master Teacher had once again convened his tutorial and, before I knew it, his robe brushed across my life as he moved to his next divine appointment.

His class convened at thirty-eight thousand feet while I read Bill McCartney's new book, *Blind Spots*. Eight hours in the air, and we were just halfway to Johannesburg. Deep in this 747's bowels were stacked our seven overstuffed suitcases. My wife, younger daughter, and I were right in the middle of moving from our beloved USA to South Africa.

In May while we were ministering in South Africa, Nigeria, and Ghana, the Lord broadsided us with traumatic hunger, famine, poverty, and AIDS. His hands gently pried open our hearts and poured in his unspeakable grief. Hot tears burned. We were unable not to go.

Now that I'm away from all distractions, the Lord returned for a follow-up teachable moment. He sought my complete attention. He had my heart, but now he called for more, much more. Passion had to deepen to burden. Blindness had to give way to sight.

But blindness can only be healed if one perceives one cannot see. In sad and profound ways, I discovered that I've been a seeing blind man.

The title *Blind Spots* turned out to be a vast understatement for this pilgrim. As the Lord led me through each chapter, guiding, convicting, and transforming, I repented in sadness and sorrow, glimpsed the truth on the other side of the Spot, and saw beyond a life of righteousness to a divine calling of justice.

Not too often does a book transform one's life, but *Blind Spots* reshaped my heart and clarified my destiny.

Thank you, good friend Bill, for pursing the dream that God planted deep in your heart. Thank you for bearing the wounds of all who have the courage to pursue their dreams in virgin forests where dragons dwell and darkness reigns.

Your breaking free of blindness and seeking reconciliation is a model for all. But perhaps most significantly of all, *Blind Spots* seeks to unite righteousness and justice at the altar of the Lord. May they embrace as one under the good hand of our God!

Thank you for your leadership, endurance, transparency, and hunger for all that God has for you. But even more, thank you for your friendship that is such a treasure and your kindred heart, which is priceless.

Assuredly, this is not your typical foreword. But now that a few blind spots have faded, perhaps it is finally time not to write a foreword but rather to live a life that moves forward. Our challenge is to move beyond the blind spots to a land you have pioneered for me and all who would desire to see the glorious land beyond human sight.

Forward, then, side by side.

DR. BRUCE WILKINSON
Author of *The Prayer of Jabez* and *Secrets of the Vine*

foreword

■　■　■　■　■

I have devoted most of my life to challenging the church of Jesus Christ in America to be reconciled to God and to one another. Without exception, bringing the church together across denominational and racial lines has been, and continues to be, the most difficult task the church faces. I have experienced a close friend and pastor taking his own life because his congregation rebelled against God's message of reconciliation. I have been beaten, jailed, and rejected because of my unrelenting stand for unity among believers in Christ. I have felt discouraged, frustrated, and alone as I preached the message of Jesus' High Priestly prayer that all of his disciples should be one.

My current condition is ecstatic joy. Why? Because my good friend and colaborer for the cause of justice and righteousness has written a must-read book—*Blind Spots*! This book is sensitive, courageous, informative, and instructive. Every pastor and church leader must have this book in his library. This book is *not* about blame—it is about brotherhood. While the growing divide in the body of Christ is specifically addressed, it doesn't stop there. This book also unveils blind spots that may hinder your marriage. Read *Blind Spots* and learn how the Coach discovered blind spots in his marriage. Apply this lesson to yourself and your congregation, and watch your own marriage and the marriages within your congregation be strengthened. We must live out this new and necessary insight regarding our blind spots, since the heart of Christ is for every believer, Jew or Gentile, to be one.

This book is not just a classic but a rare gem that every concerned pastor and leader must have.

DR. JOHN M. PERKINS
Founder/President, John Perkins Foundation
for Reconciliation & Development
Jackson, Mississippi

foreword

■ ■ ■ ■ ■

Blind Spots is a book for anyone bold enough to confront the issue of spiritual myopia. The individual who is willing to open his or her heart will hear what the Spirit of God has to say in this area. This book is a must-read for present-day leaders and emerging ones alike.

It is essential that all of us maintain a right relationship with God, for from this relationship flows a godly perspective, a profound comprehension, and a divine orientation that gives us the strength to do what is right. The church in America is in desperate need of God's sustenance.

The content of this book is realistic and personal, which makes it ideal for group study. The purpose of this book is obvious—to open our eyes and identify blind spots. And once we've identified them, to deal with them with the help of God.

As a member of the ethnic community, I have great hopes that this insightful book will promote mutual understanding in the process of including ethnic communities as essential partners in the kingdom of God in America. This process, however, must be immersed in prayer so that we may obtain enlightenment from our Lord Jesus Christ. He alone can expose our deepest inadequacies and give us the courage to make changes.

Blind Spots will enlarge your vision for diversity and unity in the body of Christ. Thanks, Coach, for taking a bold stand!

May the church in America capture your passion for biblical unity.

REV. DANIEL DE LEON
Senior Pastor, Templo Calvario
Santa Ana, California
Member, Promise Keepers Board of Directors

acknowledgments

■ ■ ■ ■ ■

I want to acknowledge individuals who contributed the most in assisting me with *Blind Spots*.

First is Steve Halliday. He took our words and thoughts and transformed them into what you will read. Rarely has anyone been able to capture my thoughts and put them into writing as this gifted warrior for our Lord. This was not simply a writing project. It became clear to me that Steve believed in *Blind Spots*.

Second, my close friend, colaborer, and "Level Four" soul mate (read chapter 8); the one who tolerates my idiosyncrasies and loves me still; the one who I know, no matter what the circumstance and situation, has got my back; my friend indeed—Raleigh Washington.

Third, I want to acknowledge Amnon Shor, Marty Waldman, David Chernoff, and Bob Cohen—Messianic Jewish rabbis who have been instrumental in helping me understand God's heart for Israel and the Jewish people.

I also want to acknowledge individuals who at various steps of the process made priceless contributions to the finished product: Dr. Tony Evans, Dr. Jack Hayford, Bishop Phillip Porter, Dr. Gordon England, Ray Vialpando, Levi Velasco, Deswood Tome, Harold Velasquez, Steve Chavis, Terry Schofield, and Jeff Leever.

A special thanks to Curtis Lundgren, senior editor at Tyndale House, who took our draft and gave input and insight that were invaluable.

introduction

■ ■ ■ ■ ■

PASTORS, GOD'S GIFT TO THE CHURCH

There was a man sent from God, whose name was John.
JOHN 1:6, NKJV

The sixth verse of the Gospel of John identifies John the Baptist as a man sent from God. I believe that if this Scripture were re-written today, it would say instead, "whose name is *your pastor.*"

Pastors are called and sent by God. No more significant a calling exists than to be called by God to shepherd the sheep of our Father's pasture.

Promise Keepers has been raised up and sustained by God to serve as a resource to the Lord's pastors. As Promise Keepers has developed, our mission has become increasingly clear, and today we have no doubt about our mission. Our "customer" is you, the pastor. We exist to help you connect with men so that you might lead them to fulfill God's call on their lives. "Promise Keepers," we often say, "is dedicated to igniting and uniting men to be passionate followers of Jesus Christ." This book is written to you (and to all spiritual leaders) for your benefit. It will address the most devastating issue confronting the church and will reveal that subtle distortions in our perceptions hide or camouflage the spiritual importance of this issue.

The Lord is longing for his sons to stop judging each other harshly and to bond in his name. Whether from experiencing pain and long-standing hurt or from defending efforts genuinely good, we have become a church of leaders who unknowingly and unintentionally slip into judging one another's motives. Actions can sting even when motives remain pure.

I'm not writing to lecture, judge, or browbeat church leaders. Far from it! For fifty-four years, while I honored and respected the church, I had no idea how it worked. I just wasn't paying attention; I was charging down another hill. When I left coaching to work with Promise Keepers, I quickly discovered that I had a lot to learn about ministry. I was appalled to see how pastors must face constant criticism, critique, and judgmentalism. God wants us to pray for, love, and support those whom he has given us as shepherds. If we constantly cut our pastor down and judge him, the result will be a scattering of the sheep, but if we pray for him and encourage him, we'll see the sheep flocking, even thriving together. "Strike the Shepherd that the sheep may be scattered" (Zech. 13:7, NASB). Sure, I'm still quite capable of slipping into a judgmental attitude toward another. I'm still learning. I have to review the basics every day. I don't claim to be anything more than saved by grace and still rough around the edges. My words are meant to encourage, to be inclusive, and to edify. If you're like me and your words often come out all wrong, then let's set a goal of building one another up and pursue it relentlessly.

I need others to help me compensate and concentrate on those things that escape my notice. I need the eyes of others to assist me in identifying and overcoming these blind spots I don't even know I have. I don't know what I don't know—but others can help me to understand.

And the same is true for the church and for the pastors and godly leaders who shepherd and lead God's people. We hope that this book will ignite pastors and leaders to respond in significant ways, resulting in dramatic, desperately needed, and permanent change in the church of Jesus Christ.

Lord willing, this volume is the first of several books. Next year Promise Keepers plans to produce a resource focused on another critical area of masculine need—marriage, perhaps, or the disconnect with the next generation. Our goal is to create one resource a year for the next several years, each volume addressing a different blind spot in a critical area of need. We see this as our calling and as an effective way to serve you, the pastor, as well as other leaders and the men of the church of Jesus Christ.

God has given us this ministry, we believe, because we spend a disproportionate amount of time with men. While our research is imperfect and we do not consider ourselves "experts," our experience has demonstrated that we seem well equipped to relate various pieces of truth to pastors and other leaders who can use this information to motivate their men.

A CALL TO ACTION—AND TO MERCY

If the church is once more to thrive in this nation and boldly advance the kingdom of God—and if her pastors and leaders are to fully experience the satisfaction and deep fulfillment that God wants them to enjoy—then, beyond all doubt, Christians must recognize and deal with the deadly assumptions, misconceptions, resentments, and unfamiliarity that we have allowed to shape our thinking, planning, and praying for too long. But if we are going to help each other to see what none of us as individuals can see, we must do it with mercy and compassion. None of us will share our deep hurts and fears if we think we're going to be rejected for doing so.

Until recently, I didn't realize that *I* had driven Jesus to the

Cross. Does that statement surprise you? As long as I compared myself to others, I felt secure. But from 1995 to 1997, I traveled to fifty-five major cities across the United States to sit at the feet of leaders who minister in urban settings. I wanted to hear their hearts. Frustration and wrath poured out of their pain, and I felt myself wincing and withdrawing from the bombardment. I was guilty on all counts: self-concerned, conceited, conditional, and manipulative. It drove me to my knees.

As I got alone with the Lord, I began to see my heart—and felt plagued by my own accusing nature. I drew no relief in those intimate moments, as Scripture verses rendered me defenseless. My pride, arrogance, performance-driven attitudes, and tunnel vision haunted me. I saw my heart riddled with selfish motives, a lack of genuine compassion, and preoccupation with my own priorities. Woe! Woe! Woe! And it got worse—perhaps it was this kind of experience that led Peter to want to be crucified upside down.

"Lord, have mercy!" I cried. "I can't defend myself. I need mercy!"

In a very real sense, this book is about mercy. In Matthew 9:13 our Lord says, "Go and learn what this means: 'I desire mercy, not sacrifice.' " I find it intriguing that three chapters later, Jesus again quotes Hosea 6:6 when he declares, "If you had known what this means, 'I desire mercy and not sacrifice,' you would not have condemned the guiltless" (Matt. 12:7, NKJV).

Brothers, we have to quit passing judgment. We have to bond in his name. We are leaders who slip unaware into condemning one another, presuming self-indulgent motives, and harboring contempt. Our blind spots have betrayed us. Jesus tells us that "he who has been forgiven little loves little" (Luke 7:47). But he who has been forgiven much, loves much. We should remember that while *God* twice called Job "blameless," the patriarch's *friends* heaped blame upon him (about thirty-four chapters' worth!). When we get to heaven and see Jesus in his glory, we'll truly discover that the mercy God provided to us far exceeded what we offered to each other. And yet Jesus says to us, "Blessed are the merciful, for they shall obtain mercy" (Matt. 5:7, NKJV).

Our Lord warns us in Matthew 24 that as the time for his return draws near, the influence of the evil one will increase and the love of many will grow cold (v. 12). *That day is here!* If we are to "occupy" until he comes (Luke 19:13, KJV), then we need each other. A house divided cannot stand, but a house held together by mercy can rescue us. It is time for us to circle the wagons and rally the church. Every man urgently needs to do his part and fulfill his God-given ministry.

Consider how Peter responded to a request for alms by a man born lame: "Silver and gold I do not have, but what I do have I give you" (Acts 3:6, NKJV). The apostle's response characterizes the spirit of the church that God birthed. The man wanted money for food, but Peter gave him something far better than money. We, too, need something better than money—and only a united church can give it to us.

Pastors, I urge you to get your men back in the game. Let's help our men discover and use their gifts. It's true that the times are difficult—but they're also exciting! By working together, we can advance God's kingdom for his glory and our benefit.

chapter one WE DON'T KNOW WHAT WE DON'T KNOW

Legend has it that several years ago a young man named John Long played football for the University of Illinois. The Fighting Illini were preparing to play the last game of the regular season at home against a tough opponent. Illinois hadn't been to the Rose Bowl in twenty years, but if the team won this game, they would be headed to Pasadena. As game day approached, a great excitement and restless energy filled the Urbana-Champaign area.

On Friday afternoon after practice, John Long approached his coach and said, "Coach, you just have to start me in tomorrow's game."

The coach looked at his player, surprised. "John," he said, "I want to tell you that as a senior, you have done everything I've ever asked you to do. You've been a

model kid, a great student. But you haven't started a game since you've been here! Furthermore, you play behind the captain of the team at your linebacker position. How can you ask, in a game of this magnitude, to be a starter?"

Tears rolled down the young man's face as he replied, "Coach, I know that's true. But you just *have* to start me."

As the pressure bore down, the bewildered coach tried to buy a little time. "Let me sleep on it," he said.

The night before a game major college teams routinely stay in a hotel to get away from all the craziness on campus. Early the next morning, John banged on his coach's door. The coach emerged from his room and said, "John, I thought about it, and here's what I'm willing to do. I'm going to put you in for the opening kickoff. That way, technically, you'll be starting the game. But I can't concede any more than that."

As fate would have it, Illinois kicked off and John Long ran down the field faster than anyone had ever seen him run. He made a tremendous tackle at about the eighteen-yard line, then jumped up with fists clenched. The team captain started to run onto the field, but the coach grabbed him and pulled him off.

"Give him one more play," he said, "because that was a great hit."

On the first play from scrimmage, the opposing quarterback pitched the ball to the tailback, who started running to the wide side of the field. He stopped, then threw back across the field to the quarterback, who was trying to slip out the back side. Somehow, from his linebacker position, Long diagnosed the play, stepped in front of the receiver, picked off the pass, and ran untouched into the end zone. Illinois missed the extra point but still led 6-0.

By now the coach *couldn't* take Long out; the kid had just scored a touchdown! In fact, he was all over the field that day, and the coach couldn't take him out at all. John Long dominated the game, and his coach eventually substituted the captain a linebacker position. The 6-0 score held up, and as the onds ticked away, pandemonium swept the stadium. A bration broke out, and the Fighting Illini carried their coach off the field. Finally the players spilled into the locker room. As the jubilant coach gathered himself, he saw John Long off in the corner, all by himself, crying like a baby. The young man wept uncontrollably.

The puzzled coach approached his distraught senior and said, "John, why are you crying? You played like no one has ever seen you play. No one has ever seen you do those things. You dominated the game. Why are you crying?"

"Coach," he replied after calming down a little, "you know that my father is blind."

"Of course I do," the coach answered. "Many times your fraternity brothers wheeled him out on the field so he could listen to us practice."

"Well, Coach," John said, "my dad died Thursday night. I figured this was the first time he had a chance to see me play."

Imagine! John Long sat on the bench for four long years, while all that time possessing the ability to dominate a football game. What kept him from reaching toward greatness?

BLIND SPOTS

John Long suffered from a blind spot—he couldn't envision how good he could be. His coach suffered from a blind spot—he didn't know how to effectively motivate this bench-sitting senior. But what if these blind spots had been identified and dealt with earlier? What might have happened?

I can't help but wonder, how many fathers have sons just like John Long sitting under their roofs? How many pastors have John Longs hibernating in their churches? I believe that thousands of John Longs sit in our pews. They're fully capable of dominating ministry areas for the glory of God—but to this point, they're content to be "saved and sittin' on it." They're benched.

But what would happen if pastors and church leaders could help these men to see their true abilities? What might occur if we learned how to effectively motivate these men to excellence? How quickly could we in the church reach the "Rose Bowl" if we identified our blind spots and took steps to overcome them?

WE NEED OTHERS

In my coaching days, we graded our assistants in four areas of effectiveness:

1. in the classroom
2. with film or video
3. on the field
4. in player relationships

We discovered that virtually no one is good at everything. A guy can be weak in the classroom but great with players. If I saw that a wide receiver coach did a poor job on the chalkboard, I would tell my offensive coordinator, "I don't want him on the board. Keep his players with yours and go over all the material on the chalkboard, and then send him straight to the field." If I thought a coach did a substandard job on film but excelled on the chalkboard, I'd say to his superior, "I don't want him showing film to the players. Have his players with you every time you turn on the projector, but let him go to town on the board." In that way we could compensate for what we saw as a coach's blind spot.

Of course, this had to be done in such a way that it didn't steal a man's dignity. Let's say a receiver coach did great on film but poorly on the field. And let's say the offensive coordinator also served as the quarterback coach. I'd just direct my offensive coordinator to say to the receiver coach, "The most effective way to develop our passing game is to do this together." That way the man was afforded the respect he deserved, and we were able to compensate for his blind spot.

I once had an assistant coach who applied for a job with the Chicago Bears, then coached by Mike Ditka. Before my assistant left for his interview, I told him, "You'd better let me talk to Ditka before you go."

I got Ditka on the phone and said, "Mike, let me tell you what you have here. If you turn on the film and watch this guy go to work, you'll see he's great. In fact, he's the best I've ever seen. He's precise. I almost want him showing film to everybody, his eye is so keen. But don't put him on the chalkboard—he'll wear you out. He doesn't do a good job of explaining things. If you put him on the chalkboard, you won't hire him. But if you put him on film, you'll hire him immediately."

Men, in particular, need others to help them compensate for their blind spots. God built a man to focus on a certain target; he reaches that target by blocking off everything else. But the same ability that allows him to succeed also leads to blind spots. And blind spots, left to themselves, lead to failure and defeat.

"Two are better than one," says Solomon in Ecclesiastes 4:9-10, "because they have a good return for their work: If one falls down, his friend can help him up. But pity the man who falls and has no one to help him up!" A friend jokingly refers to this text as the "belt and suspenders" verse. What a great picture of the safety we need when we could "lose it" because of our blind spots. Our vision doesn't show that our belt is undone, yet having another friend fill in the perspective is like suspenders holding things up—even keeping us from embarrassment.

If we are humble enough to accept someone's input, we can avoid stumbling along while we don't know what we don't know.

Dave Wardell, the cofounder of Promise Keepers, is quite an

outdoorsman. He illustrates the blind-spot problem by comparing the field of vision of hunters using different optical aids. A hunter using a three-by-nine scope on a high-powered rifle has a myopic perspective. When the crosshairs in the scope are lined up, he's right on the target, but he's totally unaware of things outside the very tight circle of vision. By contrast, a hunter using an open-bore or improved cylinder shotgun for skeet shooting or small-bird hunting sees with much more. The contrast is myopic focus versus broad peripheral vision.

THE PLAGUE OF BLIND SPOTS

Blind spots are a lot like hepatitis C, a deadly disease caused by the HCV virus, nicknamed "the stealth virus." This germ "can lie dormant in the bloodstream for decades," leaving millions of victims unaware they're infected.[1] Scientists estimate that about 170 million individuals worldwide have the HCV virus, about four times the number infected by HIV (HIV is the virus thought to cause AIDS). Nearly 85 percent of those who contract the HCV virus have it for life, and 20 percent of them develop cirrhosis, which can lead to cancer or liver failure. "By the end of the decade," says *Newsweek* magazine, "the death toll from hep C is expected to triple in the United States."[2]

Doctors identified the stealth virus fourteen years ago, but by then it had long since spread around the planet. Egypt has the highest rate of infection in the world—the HCV virus afflicts fully 15 to 25 percent of the Egyptian population—but America has definitely not escaped. Even television star Pamela Anderson and country singer Naomi Judd announced that they have the virus. Closer to home, a year ago the father of a friend of mine discovered that he has the disease; he probably contracted it decades ago from a blood transfusion.

Blind spots and the HCV virus have at least three lethal traits in common:

1. They afflict individuals of every cultural and ethnic group.
2. They work silently, without the victim's knowledge.
3. They can cause staggering damage, even death.

Blind spots kill.

We all know we need to pay special attention to a vehicle's blind spot, the area that restricts our field of vision. Until car manufacturers make a totally transparent automobile, every vehicle is going to have its blind spots, where opaque metal or plastic blocks the driver from seeing all that he or she needs to see. To drive safely, the driver must remain aware of a car's blind spots, look two or three times, and move his head to compensate. And what happens when he doesn't?

Honk! SCREECH! Crash!!

Unfortunately, blind spots affect more than cars. All of us have personal blind spots. One man recently told me that his child scored a perfect twenty-twenty on vision tests—but still couldn't read properly. Somehow the boy left words out of sentences. He had a "blind spot" for certain words, or words in certain parts of a sentence. Even those with perfect vision can still have blind spots.

BLIND SPOTS TAKE MANY FORMS

Perhaps you've seen the following old object lesson. What phrase do you read?

Paris in the
the spring

Many will read the phrase, "Paris in the spring"—but that's not what it says. The full phrase repeats the "the," leaving, "Paris in the *the* spring." Didn't see it before? That's because we all have a tendency to see what we think is right, rather than what is actually there in front of us.

Another little phenomenon is the blind spot. The tenth edition of *Merriam-Webster's Collegiate Dictionary* defines a *blind spot* as "1a: the nearly circular light-colored area at the back of the retina where the optic nerve enters the eyeball and which is not sensitive to light—called also *optic disk;* b: a portion of a field that cannot be seen or inspected with available equipment; 2: an area in which one fails to exercise judgment or discrimination."

This may surprise you even more. Look at the X and the O below.

Now shut your left eye and, using only your right eye, look intently at the *X.* Can you see the *O* on the right? Don't attempt to glance over at it; simply be aware that it is there in your peripheral vision. (If this isn't working, you're probably just a little too close to the page. Move back a foot or so and you should immediately be able to see the *O.*) Now slowly come back toward the page, again, looking intently at the *X.* When you're about a foot away, the *O* will disappear! In order to see it again, you have to come closer to the page. The *O* disappears because you're in the perfect position not to see it. You can do the same thing in reverse with your other eye.

We all have these blind spots, but we remain unaware unless we find out from each other. Our mind replenishes the empty space (the cavity in our vision) with whatever the surrounding background looks like. We don't see anything warning us that something important is missing from our field of vision. At that moment we are completely vulnerable.

The term *blind spots* can be used to describe far more than a lack of physical sight. I heard one expert define a personal blind spot as "a coping mechanism for the purpose of self-defense, which originates from a neurosis. If one can't cope with an issue, then one tends to act as though it's not there. After repeatedly blocking it out, it will appear to go away—but no, it remains and remains and remains." Blind spots can form in order to shield a person from the fear and anxiety that result from a neurotic or distorted understanding of reality.

Blind spots. While everybody has them, few of us can name our own. That's why we need others around us to identify our blind spots and help us compensate for them. We ignore them at our own risk. The results can be similar to neglecting important instructions from our boss or dismissing a phone message from the IRS.

The truth is, some of us just don't *want* to see certain things. They make us uncomfortable, they cause us to squirm, they make us feel guilty—and so we block them out of our sight. What do we end up with? A blind spot. But does the thing we don't want to see go away? No. Can it still hurt us? Yes.

I've developed my own definition of a blind spot: *You don't know what you don't know.* Sometimes we don't see certain things simply because we don't know to look for them. They may, in fact, cause us tremendous problems, but if no one makes us aware of their presence, we'll continue to miss them—and they'll continue to hurt us.

Scripture addresses this idea of blind spots. The apostle Paul tells us in 1 Corinthians 13:12, "Now we see but a poor reflection as in a mirror; then we shall see face to face. Now I know in part; then I shall know fully, even as I am fully known." In other words, so long as we live in these old bodies on this old earth, we'll suffer from faulty vision. The day is indeed coming when God will remove every one of our blind spots—but that day isn't yet.

An Old Testament verse adds an intriguing perspective to this. "For God does speak—now one way, now another—though man may not perceive it," says Job 33:14. In order to catch everything that God wants to say to me, I find that I have to keep my head on a swivel. I have to keep my eyes and ears open at all times. I have to be listening and on alert everywhere I go, because God is liable to speak to me anywhere. God can speak through a circumstance, through a newspaper, through a fellow Christian, through his Word. Of course, when he speaks in a way other than through his Word, I always measure it by his Word. If I think the Lord will speak to me in only one or two ways—ways that meet with my approval, of course—I'm sure to ruin my spiritual vision. I'll walk around with enough blind spots to guarantee a brutal crash.

Believe me, I speak from experience.

A BIG BLIND SPOT

I know something of the devastating power of blind spots, because a big one almost destroyed my marriage.

In 1994 I was the head football coach at the University of Colorado in Boulder. We had a great team that year with probably more talent than any other team in the nation. We ended the season at 11-1, ranked third in the country. But by October, we had yet to lose—and I was riding high.

One Sunday at church, our pastor announced that a guest speaker would deliver the following week's sermon. The man had been preaching for forty-one years, he said, had written twelve books, and had traveled the world expounding God's Word. The speaker promised to tell us the single most important thing he had learned in almost half a century of ministry.

The announcement seized my attention. I had always considered our pastor an exceptional preacher in his own right—and even *he* planned to be present the next week. So far as I knew, such a thing had never happened; guest speakers came only when our pastor planned to be out of town. *My goodness,* I thought, *this guy must be good.*

The following Saturday our football team won again, continuing its battle for the top spot in the country. Everything seemed to be going great. I arrived at church on Sunday thinking, *What could this guy preach that's the single most important thing he's learned in forty-one years?*

I didn't have to wait long to find out. The guest preacher, Jack Taylor, stepped in front of the podium and said, "Do you want to know about a man? Do you want to know whether a man has character? All you need to do is to look into his wife's countenance. Everything that he's invested or withheld will be in her face."

Jack took us from Genesis to Revelation, proving from Scripture that Almighty God has commanded every man to bring his wife to splendor in Jesus Christ. Never before had I heard of such a thing.

I turned toward my wife, Lyndi. At that time we had been married more than thirty years. And I didn't see splendor in her face; I saw torment. I didn't see contentment; I saw anguish.

I turned back to the preacher and silently complained, *He's saying that I don't have character!* But how could that be? We were filling stadiums! We were winning! And wasn't everybody saying what a great guy I was?

Yet this speaker's point hit me hard! I was actually someone very different from whom I appeared to be, even in my own estimation. His remarkable sermon laid me open, raw and exposed, as a man without character. I had a blind spot as big as my whole relationship with my wife.

For the next two weeks I tried to defend myself. I rationalized, *But I have to do this or that. It's my job!* Eventually I came to realize that my marriage had been almost exclusively about *my* dreams. We had always championed *my* goals. We had always put *my* agenda on the front burner. God, through Jack Taylor, was calling every husband to present his wife to Jesus Christ, clothed in righteousness.

Yet there sat my wife, hurting.

After an intense internal struggle, I finally decided to resign my job at the end of the season. I resolved that my wife *would* have the righteousness and splendor that God had ordained for her. Yet I had a problem. The job wouldn't be easy. I was still the same guy—selfish, inward focused, and insensitive. Reluctantly I realized that in order to become this different person of character, my old self would have to die.

Seven years after I left college football, my wife gave me a remarkable Valentine's Day card. I ought to have it framed; it says it all—but *I* won't. (It's for my eyes only; you'll just have to guess.) After seven years, the sparkle in Lyndi's eyes, the bounce in her step, the exuberance in her spirit—it all came back. In essence, she was saying to me, "You're the guy I thought I married."

In reality, I finally became a man . . . a man of character.

I had spent most of our married life convinced that by providing for my family's physical needs, by climbing the professional totem pole, I was doing my job as a husband and father. But that Sunday morning the Lord spoke to my heart, saying, "That's not where it is." For years I hadn't understood that God wants husbands and fathers to put themselves aside in order to put others first. A huge blind spot prevented me from seeing the wreck I was making of my marriage. I didn't know what I didn't know—and my ignorance cost me dearly.

Blind spots kept me from honoring and exalting my wife as God had intended. Blind spots kept me from knowing what God required of me. Not until God sent a fresh pair of eyes into my life did I see what I had never seen. It took a guest preacher standing up and saying, "This is the single most important thing I've learned in forty-one years of preaching" to take the veil off for me.

And my life has never been the same.

THE CHURCH'S BIGGEST BLIND SPOT

I believe that blind spots can afflict the church just as severely as individuals. We don't know what we don't know—and what we don't know can (and frequently does) hurt us.

It doesn't take a genius to figure out that the American church has fallen on hard times. If, as the pollsters tell us, it's true that:

- 1 percent of churches are growing
- 4 percent of our (churched) teens are saved
- 54 percent of Christian marriages end in divorce
- 20 percent of pastors have a child addicted to alcohol or drugs
- 40 percent of pastors admit involvement in Internet pornography
- 90 percent of pastors admit they're discouraged

—then the church is in very serious straights.

Why are so many pastors burned out? Why are so many men not connected in any significant way to the church or its ministries? And how did we get into such a terrible mess? I'm convinced it's because of blind spots. We don't know what we don't know.

But what is it that we don't know? It isn't that we don't know that very few of our young people are embracing a real and life-transforming faith. It isn't that we don't know how many friends and loved ones are getting divorced. No, we know these are problems, but there is a more insidious, more treacherous blind spot that we don't know about.

What you don't know is similar to driving an SUV that—unknown to you—has defective tires. You may be aware that the cars in the other lane are moving in and out of your blind spot and you may even be watching carefully to avoid hitting them. Nevertheless, if the tires blow and your SUV flips and rolls suddenly, it won't matter how careful you were. Something you didn't anticipate will have hurt you. That is the kind of thing I'm talking about.

In my work with Promise Keepers over the past several years, I've crisscrossed this nation. I've spoken with thousands of Christian men and interacted with hundreds of pastors from all denominations, representing dozens of ethnic communities. Do you know what I see as the biggest problem with the American church? It's this: *the growing divide in the church.*

Just like the defective plies that separate to weaken a tire, this deadly blind spot enables a gap to widen between Jewish and Gentile believers, between urban and suburban disciples, between conservative and charismatic Christians, between ethnic and Anglo followers of Christ. We dare not forget our Lord's stern warning that every "house divided against itself will not stand" (Matt. 12:25, NKJV). And we need to strive for the kind of powerful unity that Jesus prayed for in his High Priestly prayer of John 17. "Holy Father, keep them and care for them—all those you have given me—so that they will be united just as we are" (John 17:11, NLT).

The experiences of Promise Keepers over the past few years have convinced us that the biggest single reason for the church's staggering lack of influence is the *growing divide* between Christians of varying ethnic, theological, and socioeconomic communities. Jesus tells us that we will enjoy our greatest outreach when those outside the church see us loving each other and working together as one (see John 13:35; 17:23). Unfortunately, we have tended to remain isolated from one another, alone, separate.

Why? What accounts for our disunity and our failure to march side by side into battle under the banner of the One Great King? I don't believe it's because of spiritual rebellion, pride, or greed. I don't think the divide continues to widen primarily because of unconcern, indifference, or fear. I think the main culprit is an undetected blind spot just like the defective tire. Or perhaps we have been infected by a stealth virus like the one mentioned earlier. We simply aren't aware of the danger we're in.

And it's killing us.

At this point, many of you disagree. May I ask—even implore—you to read on? If you consider the full message before drawing conclusions, I'm convinced that God will show you what the church at large has missed.

THE DREAM REVIVED

When Dr. Martin Luther King, Jr., delivered his famous "I Have a Dream" speech back on August 28, 1963, he did so from the steps of the Lincoln Memorial in Washington, D.C. He gave his profound message to the culture at large, not to the church. Why?

Because the church couldn't hear it.

Yet Dr. King's dream came right out of God's heart. When King declared his hope that, one day, "little black boys and little black girls will be able to join hands with little white boys and white girls and walk together as sisters and brothers," he echoed the message of the Bible: "There is neither Jew nor Greek, slave nor free, male nor female, for you are all one in Christ Jesus" (Gal. 3:28). When he said that he would not be satisfied "until justice rolls down like waters and righteousness like a mighty stream," he echoed God's own words (see Amos 5:24). And when he urged his colleagues to "continue to work with the faith that unearned suffering is redemptive," he reflected an apostle's message to his friends: "Now I rejoice in what was suffered for you, and I fill up in my flesh what is still lacking in regard to Christ's afflictions, for the sake of his body, which is the church" (Col. 1:24).

Even though Dr. King spoke the very words of God from God's own heart, the church was conspicuous by its absence. When Dr. King landed in jail, few visited him. When he was slandered, no one came to stand with him. He received no support from a united church—and those who knew him best identify this failure as his single biggest disappointment. He could not believe that he spoke out of God's heart . . . and the church ignored him.

The culture heard his message and tried to respond, but the culture can never bring truth to fruition. It can do something, but in the end its efforts will inevitably fall short. And I can't help but wonder: What would have happened if the church—Jew and Gentile, urban and suburban, conservative and charismatic, ethnic and Anglo *together*—had united to honor a message straight out of God's own heart?

Of course, I know that many Christians kept their distance from Dr. King because they questioned his righteousness (see more on this concept in chapter 3). They couldn't bring themselves to align with him because they doubted his relationship with God. They couldn't listen to his words because they felt unsure he was right with God.

But had they looked out of both eyes—had they recognized a major blind spot that kept them from seeing all that God wanted them to see—they would have acknowledged the scripturally sound justice component of Dr. King's message. They would have gone to him in a biblical way and dealt lovingly with the righteousness issue. But instead, they judged him . . . and stayed away in droves.

An assassin's bullet struck down Dr. King on April 4, 1968, while he spoke from a balcony at the Lorraine Motel in Memphis, Tennessee. But his dream did not die with him. That dream flowed from the very heart of God and therefore is still very much alive.

We believe that dream is being revived today—but this time the church can embrace the dream. Last time the culture did what it could, but because it lacked the indwelling Spirit of almighty God, its labors came up short. Paul says that God "is able to do immeasurably more than all we ask or imagine." How? "According to his power *that is at work within us*" (Eph. 3:20, emphasis added). And who is the "us"? Not the culture, but the church. So the apostle concludes, "To him be glory *in the church*" (v. 21, emphasis added).

Only the church has the power to bring God's dream to fruition. Only the church has the capacity to spiritually discern the heart and desire of God.

The question is, will we discern? Will we have the appetite for God's dream? I say we will. I say it's a new day. Forty years ago the church couldn't handle God's dream. Now it can. I believe that God is doing something special among us. He's been preparing us for this day.

A VISION OF PERFECTION

The excitement I feel both for this message and the title of this book stems from a great quote by football coaching legend Don Shula. I never believed that I had anything to say on the topic of blind spots until the Lord reminded me of Shula's insightful words.

Coach Shula won 347 games, a winning percentage of .665. He took six teams to the Super Bowl, winning twice. His 1972 Miami Dolphins went 17-0, the only undefeated team in NFL history. He won the league's Coach of the Year honor four times and is so far ahead of his closest rival (in games won) that anyone within a hundred victories of him will never coach long enough to break his record; they're already too old to have any hope of catching the leader.

Shula laid out his coaching philosophy in terms that I believe can aid church leaders. "Conviction-driven leadership," he said, "is based on a vision of perfection."

What did he mean? He meant that leaders must be able to see their goal clearly and then never compromise it. Because Shula knew what he was after, he required his players to "do it the very time. He treated his players with respect, but he compromise on his vision. That made him a tremen- r.

hula knew that he couldn't see everything. He knew he had blind spots. So what did he do? He put highly competent people around him to watch for the things he couldn't see. Shula hired guys with perspectives different from his own but who bought into his vision. As a result, he was way ahead of the game. He left no detail hanging—and that enabled him to succeed like no one else.

All of us urgently need one another. Don Shula knew the importance of everyone pulling together, and he won 347 games because of it. He knew he couldn't reach his vision of perfection without the help of others who saw things he couldn't.

We're persuaded that the vision of perfection God has for his church cannot be attained without *all* the members working closely together—urban and suburban, black and white, Native American, Hispanic, Asian, Messianic Jew, and everyone else— for the advancement and expansion of the kingdom.

LET'S TALK—THEN ACT

We all have blind spots. It's time that we acknowledge them, ask for help, and begin to see some of the things we have not yet seen—even if that makes us uncomfortable. If we are to experience God's vision of perfection for his church, we not only have to work together, we have to *risk* working together.

"Life is either a daring adventure or it is nothing," Helen Keller declared. "In order to discover new lands, one must first commit to losing sight of shore for a very long time," said Andre Gide. "A ship in a harbor is safe," agreed William Shedd, "but that is not what ships are built for."

God did not build the church for our safety but to equip us to win at spiritual warfare. He calls us to "demolish strongholds" and to "demolish arguments and every pretension that sets itself up against the knowledge of God" and to "take captive every thought to make it obedient to Christ" (2 Cor. 10:4-5). Jesus said that he would build his church in such a way that "the gates of Hades will not overcome it" (Matt. 16:18). Everywhere we look in the New Testament, we see images of war and battle, not comfort and ease. Paul instructed Timothy in the gospel so that his protégé might "fight the good fight" (1 Tim. 1:18; 6:12). The apostle encouraged the Ephesians to "put on the full armor of God, so that when the day of evil comes, you may be able to stand your ground, and after you have done everything, to stand" (Eph. 6:13). And at the end of his own life, Paul could say, "I have fought the good fight" (2 Tim. 4:7).

But we can't fight the battle effectively if we don't first deal with our blind spots. Casualties run high when we don't see the enemy coming. We can't expect our churches to grow, our pastors to thrive, our teens to serve the Lord, and our marriages to triumph if we don't ask our brothers and sisters to help us overcome our blind areas.

Have you ever heard of a "reticular activating system"? It's based on the idea that we don't recognize the presence of a thing until we look for it. Once we begin to look for it, however, we find it—many times, everywhere we turn our heads. Suppose you buy a new car. You never noticed the model . . . until you bought one. Now you see it all over the place. That's the reticular activating system at work.

I believe that God is beginning to put the church's reticular activating system into overdrive. He is shining heaven's searchlight on a blind spot that has caused us pain and suffering and grief for far too long. To heal the divide in the church is to heal the church.

So then—what blind spots contribute to the growing divide? Let's take a look. Together.

chapter two
THE CORE ISSUE

Back in 1989 I asked my pastor, James Ryle, to serve as chaplain for the football team at the University of Colorado. Pastor Ryle is a gifted and consecrated speaker who preaches with clarity and knows how to use good illustrations. In the past we had used various guest preachers to give chapel messages before games, but we never had recruited a permanent chaplain. While Pastor Ryle felt excited about the opportunity, he also confessed to a little apprehension.

One hot August day he came running out to the field during one of our two-a-day practice sessions. Now, two-a-days are very organized and operate on a precise schedule; coaches take great care to minimize distractions. For that reason, the pastor's presence on the field irritated me. I considered it inappropriate. *How*

would he like me rushing up to the pulpit during his sermon to say, "Pastor, I need to talk to you about something"? I wondered.

I didn't want to acknowledge Pastor Ryle at all. I saw him coming but tried to ignore him. When it became clear he had no intention of backing off, I began moseying over to him, trying to show my deep frustration every step of the way. By the time I reached him, he could hardly contain himself. The night before, he said, he had a dream in which Colorado went undefeated—and I won national Coach of the Year.

Suddenly I paid him a good deal more attention.

As it turned out, everything that he described happened. We went 11-0 in the regular season, losing only to Notre Dame in the Orange Bowl. (He didn't say that we'd win the national championship, only that we'd go undefeated—and we did, during the regular season.) And I won Coach of the Year honors.

The next year we had a lot of our top players back, so we thought we could again contend for the national championship. But after the first three games of the season, we stood at an indifferent 1-1-1. On the road to Austin one Tuesday before we played a powerhouse Texas team, I got up early to read the Bible. Before long I stopped abruptly at the eleventh verse of Isaiah 11: "It shall come to pass in that day that the Lord shall set His hand again the second time to recover the remnant of His people who are left" (NKJV).

In that moment, the Holy Spirit seemed to bring the text alive for me. I perceived that God was telling me he was about to repeat for our football team what he had done the previous year. And that's exactly what happened. We went 11-1-1—mirroring the verse number of Isaiah 11:11—and the Associated Press voted us national champions.

There's a wholly different feeling when you know ahead of time that you're going to win. Yet when someone tells you in advance what's about to happen, you realize that it doesn't happen because of *you*. It's a God thing.

The Lord forever marked me through that experience. I learned that God always does what he says he'll do, however unlikely it may seem. At the same time, I also started to develop a burden for the "remnant" of his chosen people whom God promises to one day recover.

A STERN WARNING ABOUT INTENSE SPIRITUAL WARFARE

Early in 1997, Promise Keepers held a pre–Stand In the Gap summit for key participants and invited four Messianic Jewish leaders to participate. They expressed great satisfaction that we had asked them to take a major role in the conferences, but they also gave us a stern warning.

"You're the first Christian organization that has ever invited us to be a part of its work," they said. "But do you understand what you're doing when you invite us as a group? You're inviting the highest order of spiritual warfare. Prepare for the brunt of a spiritual attack."

The relationship between believing Jews and Gentiles carries such enormous biblical significance that Satan concentrates much of hell's firepower on trying to keep the two groups separate, apart, and alienated. He knows that if he can keep us estranged, he will have a much easier job keeping all other groups divided.

Even beyond that, Satan has always stoked a special hatred for the Jews, the chosen people of God, for through them the Messiah came to "destroy" the devil (Heb. 2:14). Ever since the Lord announced that he would send a Savior into the world, Satan has tried to wipe out the people through whom that Savior would come. It is not mere coincidence that wicked Queen Athaliah managed to wipe out all of David's male descendants, except for one (see 2 Kings 11:1-2). Nor is it a coincidence that vile Haman tried to exterminate all the Jews throughout Persia (see Esther 3:6) or that the evil King Herod tried to do the same thing to all the infant boys in Bethlehem after Jesus was born there (see Matt. 2:16).

Even after Satan failed in his many attempts to annihilate the Jews (and with them, the Messiah), he continued to nurture a furious rage against God's chosen people. He nurtures it still.

The book of Revelation declares how the devil even today continues to hound and attack and try to snuff out the chosen people of God. It pictures Israel as a woman who gave birth to Jesus Christ and says that Satan "persecuted the woman who gave birth to the male Child" (Rev. 12:13, NKJV). The devil knows that the Jews remain the chosen people of God and that the Lord will one day draw all his people to himself. Satan especially despises all of God's chosen who commit themselves to faith in Jesus Christ, and so Revelation describes how the devil "was enraged with the woman, and he went to make war with the rest of her offspring, who keep the commandments of God and have the testimony of Jesus Christ" (Rev. 12:17, NKJV).

Wherever he can do so, Satan inspires intense hatred against God's chosen people. On September 11, 2001, America found out how intense that hatred can burn. On that day, terrorists destroyed the World Trade Center towers in New York and part of the Pentagon in Washington, D.C., largely because of the support the United States has given to Israel through the years. The devil makes war not only against "the rest of her [Israel's] offspring," but against any who dare to stand with them. Our Messianic Jewish friends warned us about the consequences of standing with them for good reason! When you get in touch with the purposes of God and work to unite believing Jews and Gentiles, you will experience the height of spiritual warfare. But when you stick with it, victory is yours.

We heard their warnings but went ahead with our invitation anyway.

The week after our Stand In the Gap event, ABC newsman Ted Koppel invited me to appear on *Nightline*, his award-winning and highly acclaimed network program. Shortly before I was to appear, I injured my back while getting some exercise at the hotel where the show was to be taped. The pain grew so intense that I didn't see how I could go on the show (by the grace of God I did appear) without some relief. The hotel doctor prescribed a strong painkiller, but his prescription produced a reaction in me very similar to an overdose, and I started to hallucinate. For three or four days I struggled with incredible emotional turmoil and tangible physical agitation. Satan was just waiting for such an opportunity, and I entered into what I have concluded was a period of intense spiritual warfare. I had to fight to keep my mind, and I have never felt so dismayed in all my life, before or since. It was horrifying. There is no doubt in my mind that the onslaught was supernatural and evil.

By the time I returned home, my wife had gone to visit family, and I found myself alone in the house. That night I grew so fearful that I called a Christian brother and asked him to stay with me. We also called many other Christian friends for prayer support.

Shortly thereafter, Promise Keepers began a nosedive. We had been filling stadiums; now we were struggling to stay alive. Internal conflicts erupted throughout our organization. When we felt God calling us to work in Israel, we spent a year doing some groundwork. It went nowhere.

I remember this season of my life as a bitterly hard time. What had happened? Had we provoked the highest order of spiritual warfare? Had we been hit with the full force of a spiritual attack? Only now am I beginning to piece together the puzzle.

Our Messianic Jewish brothers had warned us that a close connection to them would result in the most intense spiritual warfare that we had ever experienced—and their words proved deadly accurate. Yet they also predicted that if we stuck with

God's leading and continued to encourage God's children to repair the growing divide in the church, we would receive a "double
blessing." We think we may be on the threshold of that blessing
right now.

Through these experiences, coupled with a close reading of
Scripture, we believe that we have identified the key to repairing
the growing divide in the church. We're convinced that we will
succeed in our efforts at reconciliation only when we focus our attention on the rift most highlighted in Scripture: the breach between believing Jews and Gentiles. All others are subordinate to
this one. Our mission is to rally the church and repair the divide.

Is this a new perspective for you? May I confess that we
didn't see it for a long time, either. A genuine blind spot! My
brothers, especially my brothers of color, please read further before drawing conclusions.

A HISTORY OF DIVISION

For the first many years of the Christian era, believing Jews made
up the vast majority of the church. Not until the time of Acts 10,
when God showed Peter that he intended to share the Good
News of Christ with the Gentile world, did the church intentionally begin to reach out to non-Jews.

We read in Acts 13 that the Holy Spirit set apart Paul and
Barnabas to take the gospel to the Gentiles. And by Acts 15, the
church had to call a historic council meeting to decide whether
Gentiles had to be circumcised and obey the law of Moses in order to be saved. The Jerusalem Council quickly endorsed Peter's
words that both Jew and Gentile were saved through the grace of
the Lord Jesus (v. 11), and the Gentiles were asked, not commanded (v. 28) to observe several essentials, later reduced to four:
abstain from idolatry; fornication; bloodshed; and abstain from
things strangled.[1]

Within a few decades, the ethnic makeup of the church

changed drastically. Largely due to the powerful ministry of Paul, converted Gentiles began to outnumber, and then overwhelmingly outnumber, their believing Jewish brethren. The trend continued for hundreds of years until the church was completely devoid of a Messianic Jewish presence. Indeed, the historic church officially rejected its Jewish roots and a Messianic Jewish influence, particularly expressed through the two Nicene church councils of the fourth and seventh centuries.

Church history reveals that by the time of the Reformation in the sixteenth century, evangelism to the Jewish people had nearly died out. In fact, prior to the Reformation the church had implemented a "forced" conversion policy toward the Jewish people. An anti-Jewish attitude in the church continued after the Reformation because Martin Luther and others expected many Jewish men and women to welcome the reformed message of the gospel. When it did not get a warm reception, Luther wrote several anti-Semitic tracts, including "Against the Jews." Throughout the following centuries, frequent pogroms (organized massacres) against Jews broke out in many European nations, often in the name of Christ. Even in the twentieth century, Adolf Hitler quoted Martin Luther to justify his efforts to exterminate the Jews. In this way, Christianity became repulsive to the vast majority of Jewish people.

Approximately thirty years ago, some of this attitude began to change in the church and there was evidence of a growing receptivity of the gospel among Jewish people. Through the efforts of groups such as Jews for Jesus, the gospel began once more to spread among the Jews. Out of this revival developed an ever-growing force called the Messianic movement. Prior to its emergence, Jews who became believers in Christ were expected to observe Christianity according to the patterns developed among Gentile believers. All customs, traditions, and actions recognized as Jewish were considered heretical or at least biblically inappropriate, as the practices were thought to relate to law rather than grace. For this reason, few Jews accepted Christ because they assumed such a choice meant giving up every tradition that marked them as Jews.

The Messianic movement, however, offered the faith of Yeshua (Jesus) without requiring anyone to give up traditions and practices that Jesus himself observed (the feast of Hanukkah, for example, is mentioned in John 10:22). This growing movement still struggles greatly for acceptance by the Gentile majority of Christendom. Most Gentile believers know little about the Messianic movement, and some who are aware write it off as a cult or as an "oddball branch of Christianity" without the courtesy of investigation.

As a result of such direct and indirect rejection, the divide in the body of Christ, which has existed since early centuries, continues to be perpetuated between believing Jews and believing Gentiles. This divide is both racial and spiritual. And while Messianic Jews probably represent the smallest segment of the body of Christ in the United States, in my view they represent the biggest spiritual dynamic. Let me tell you why.

After seventeen centuries of the absence of Messianic Jews in the church, God is beginning to restore the Messianic Jewish community (the Church of the Circumcision) to the body of Christ. This revival of the gospel among Jewish people is unprecedented apart from the book of Acts. The Jewish revival is nothing short of a miracle and certainly represents the work of the Holy Spirit in preparation for the return of Jesus Christ. One of the major issues that faces the church today is its receptivity toward our Jewish brethren. Our brothers, the Messianic Jews, have been rejected by their own community for their faith in Jesus, the Messiah. Rather than receiving this community of Jewish believers with enthusiasm and love, the church has viewed them with suspicion and reluctance.

One way to illustrate this point is through the analogy of the olive tree used in Romans 11. The Jewish branches that were cut off because of unbelief are now returning to their own olive tree. The wild olives (Gentiles) that were grafted in to the Jewish tree because of their belief have occupied this tree for seventeen centuries without much thought of the natural branches. They also have forgotten that they were grafted in. With the return of the natural branches, the grafted-in branches feel some discomfort and embarrassment and even unbelief.

This can be compared to the owner of a home welcoming strangers into his home just before leaving on a long journey. When the original owner returns after such a long absence, it is very difficult for the original strangers, who have now come to accept this home as their sole possession, to accept that they need to make room for the original owner and even to give him the place of honor. It is likewise difficult for the original owner to return and find that there is little room for him in his own house and that he must now conform to the strangers' ways. It is only by God's grace that any of us occupy any part of God's house, but Scripture tells us to give "honor to whom honor is due" (Rom. 13:7, NRSV). Personally, I rejoice in the return of my elder brothers of the Messianic Jewish community.

TEARING DOWN THE DIVIDING WALL

Do you like a good mystery? The Bible does, although it uses the term *mystery* more to describe a long-hidden secret, now revealed.

The apostle Paul uses the word *mystery* to refer to a divine secret that "in other ages was not made known to the sons of men, as it has now been revealed by the Spirit to His holy apostles and prophets" (Eph. 3:5, NKJV). And what is this mystery? Just this: "that through the gospel the Gentiles are heirs together with Israel, members together of one body, and sharers together in the promise in Christ Jesus" (v. 6).

Paul proclaimed that God had commissioned him as an apostle "to make plain to everyone the administration of this mystery, which for ages past was kept hidden in God" (v. 9). And what was God's purpose in revealing this mystery? What did he hope to accomplish? Paul answers, "His intent was that now, through the church, the manifold wisdom of God should be made known to the rulers and authorities in the heavenly realms" (v. 10).

God did not want to create two church bodies but one. He had no intention of creating one church for Jews and a separate one for Gentiles. He planned for both ethnic groups to come together as one, in a single body, and thereby show the powers of heaven the depth and breadth of his awesome wisdom. We do not diminish today's intense struggles between Anglo, African American, Hispanic, Asian, and Native American believers; rather, we believe there is a core issue in The Great Divide.

Paul did not want his Gentile friends to forget what an astonishing thing God had done to pull off such a miracle. The apostle reminded them what they were formerly:

> *You were separate from Christ, excluded from citizenship in Israel and foreigners to the covenants of the promise, without hope and without God in the world. But now in Christ Jesus you who once were far away have been brought near through the blood of Christ. For he himself is our peace, who has made the two one and has destroyed the barrier, the dividing wall of hostility, by abolishing in his flesh the law with its commandments and regulations. His purpose was to create in himself one new man out of the two, thus making peace, and in this one body to reconcile both of them to God through the cross, by which he put to death their hostility. (Eph. 2:12-16)*

At Calvary, Jesus broke down the dividing wall of hostility between Jew and Gentile in order to make both groups one, thus establishing peace. The Bible therefore gives no warrant for the growing divide between these two groups of believers.

TOP BUTTON ON THE SHIRT OF CHRISTIAN UNITY

The apostle continues his thoughts on mysteries in Romans 10–11. There he tells his friends that God has saved the Gentiles "to make Israel envious" (11:11). He adds, "I do not want you to be ignorant of this mystery, brothers, so that you may not be conceited: Israel has experienced a hardening in part until the full number of the Gentiles has come in. And so all Israel will be saved" (11:25-26).

Paul does not want Gentile believers to look down on unbelieving Jews because they have so far missed the grace of God in Christ. Instead, he encourages them to live in such a way that God's chosen people will see and receive the riches available in Jesus. Paul himself says, "I make much of my ministry in the hope that I may somehow arouse my own people to envy and save some of them" (11:13-14).

This is God's declared plan for the church. But how can we provoke Jewish men or women to envy if we have no relationship with them? And how can we reach unbelieving Jews if we don't even have a relationship with believing Jews? I strongly believe that this is the core reconciliation issue facing the church today.

The growing divide between believing Jews and Gentiles violates Scripture and is a huge spiritual problem. Except where profound theological differences separate believers, virtually all of the rest of the divisions in the body are relational, whether they involve Latinos, African Americans, Asians, Native Americans, whites, denominational concerns, or other issues. While Scripture speaks to all divisions, the relationship between believing Jews and Gentiles is specifically addressed. The most critical divide, the one to be addressed first, is this growing rift.

It's not a good idea to put on a shirt by fastening the middle buttons first. When you do, the frequent result is misalignment. If, however, you begin by fastening the top buttonhole, all the other buttons and holes line up perfectly. I believe that the relationship between believing Jews and Gentiles is the top button on the shirt of Christian unity.

SOMETHING BROKE

Recent events have convinced me that the Lord has been preparing us all along to encourage and help the church to come together as one. I have known for a long time that Promise Keepers is a peacemaking ministry, and I am starting to see more clearly how God may want this ministry to help bring his sons together.

Just a few days ago I returned home from a Messianic Jewish conference at which I gave a short message. My Jewish friends introduced me like this: "No one has reached out to us in seventeen hundred years like Promise Keepers."

Just before I delivered my message, I felt tremendous spiritual warfare raging all around—and then tremendous peace. God used it to show me that this work of reconciliation is the most important thing we have ever done. Something broke that day in the heavenlies. What happens next is going to change the church. I know it in my heart.

This important focus on reconciliation between Messianic Jewish believers and Gentile believers is a new priority for all of us here at Promise Keepers. I have prayed earnestly about its significance and asked God to show me the best way to approach it. I'm still in the process of figuring out the best approach.

In the meantime, we'll continue our ongoing work of reconciling different ethnic groups, emphasizing the divide between the urban and suburban church. Some of the material in this book, such as the material regarding the disconnect between justice and righteousness, the ideas about building intimate relationships, and the encouragement to humbly listen and really hear each other, is specific to that situation. Much of it can be applied to any division or misunderstanding pastors find within their own church or community.

God is orchestrating marvelous things in our day. And when he orchestrates them in advance, we get no credit—I learned that lesson years ago as a football coach. I'm neither a prophet nor the son of a prophet, but I believe I can see something of what God plans to do among us.

In Matthew 24, Jesus predicts that the influence of the evil one will vastly increase in the last days. He says that the love of most Christians will grow cold *because* of an increase in lawlessness (v. 12). I believe that God is choosing this time to bring together believing Jews and Gentiles so that we may triumph in this dark day. Together we have enough power and resources to advance God's kingdom—but not if we remain fragmented.

Promise Keepers, we often say, "is dedicated to igniting and uniting men to be passionate followers of Jesus Christ." Our mission is and always has been to ignite and unite; but while the first is happening, the second is not. The first key to uniting, the secret to becoming the formidable force God wants us to be, is linking up with the Messianic Jewish community. And when that happens, says Paul, "through the church, the manifold wisdom of God should be made known to the rulers and authorities in the heavenly realms" (Eph. 3:10).

Meanwhile, we on earth will reap untold blessings.

chapter three

MAKE ROOM IN YOUR HEART

A few weeks ago Raleigh Washington, my good friend and colleague here at Promise Keepers, and I flew to Los Angeles to meet with an influential Christian leader. We had made all the arrangements for our meeting well in advance. We bought our plane tickets, flew to LA, picked up a rental car, drove to the specified meeting place . . . and the guy didn't show up. No explanation. No phone call. No apology. He just didn't show up.

I've been dealing with this issue ever since. What did we do to prompt him to skip the meeting? Apparently, somebody at our headquarters didn't return a phone call. I thought he must have felt slighted and so snubbed us by boycotting our visit.

Everything in me wanted to retaliate. I wanted to say, "How can you let me fly all the way to *your* city, and then, because somebody didn't return a phone call, you decide

not to show up—and you don't even tell us that you're not going to come? How can you do that and still call yourself a Christian?"

Don't get me wrong—I think this issue must be confronted. Anything less would reveal a serious lack of integrity on my part. What I can't do is explode. What wouldn't help is to read this guy the riot act and then storm away. I have to find a way to confront the issue but do so in a way that safeguards the man's dignity and tries to understand his perspective.

In other words, I have to make room in my heart for him. The apostle Paul wrote,

> *Make room for us in your hearts. We have wronged no one, we have corrupted no one, we have exploited no one. I do not say this to condemn you; I have said before that you have such a place in our hearts that we would live or die with you. I have great confidence in you; I take great pride in you. I am greatly encouraged; in all our troubles my joy knows no bounds. (2 Cor. 7:2-4)*

Here's the kicker: I did confront the issue and resolved the matter in biblical fashion, only to learn that it involved a serious breakdown of communication, not intent. No relationship can long endure, let alone thrive, if its members don't consciously and continually make room in their hearts for one another. Yes, we will be slighted. Yes, we will be disappointed. Yes, we will be misunderstood. But unless we develop the habit of making room in our hearts—especially for those from cultures and backgrounds different from our own—we have no chance of coming together as God wants us to.

THE KEY COMPONENT
What is required for God's sons and daughters to come together as one? What's the key component in making room in our hearts?

In my view, it comes down to one thing: deep humility, expressed through a heart of loving-kindness.

I can't sing—I can't even carry a tune—but I love the song that proclaims, "Justice flows like a river when God's sons are clothed in humility." How do you get deep humility? You have to clothe yourself in it. You have to put it on. You have to wear it.

"And so," Paul writes, "as those who have been chosen of God, holy and beloved, *put on* a heart of compassion, kindness, *humility*, gentleness and patience; bearing with one another, and forgiving each other, whoever has a complaint against anyone, just as the Lord forgave you" (Col. 3:12-13, NASB, emphasis added).

The apostle Peter agrees with his colleague Paul. "You younger men," he writes, "be subject to your elders; and all of you, *clothe yourselves with humility toward one another*, for God is opposed to the proud, but gives grace to the humble" (1 Pet. 5:5, NASB, emphasis added).

Why do we have to clothe ourselves with deep humility when we say to someone, "Come near to me"? I'll tell you why. Some men have been so hurt by what life has served up that they distrust any show of concern or personal interest from anyone belonging to another ethnic group. You couldn't get them to come to a "reconciliation meeting" if you sent a limo, made first-class arrangements, and put them up at the Waldorf. And yet, they effectively share the gospel in their communities. Could they be more effective? Yes—if they had some help and support. That's why it's so crucial that we say to one another, "Come near to me." But in order for that to happen, we absolutely must make room in our hearts.

The fact that we have blind spots requires that we develop deep humility. All of us see in a mirror, dimly. Each of us needs the Holy Spirit and others to help us see what we can't see on our own. Alone, each of us will fall into a pit. God is searching for humble pastors and church leaders who will model deep humility.

And how do we develop such humility? First, we remember that God says he chose us (see John 15:16; 1 Pet. 2:9), "not because of anything we have done but because of his own purpose and grace" (2 Tim. 1:9). When we understand that we have received grace (and not earned a paycheck), how can anything but deep humility follow?

Second, we need to honestly evaluate ourselves and our records. Honest self-assessment naturally leads to humility. Jesus told us not to look at the toothpick in our brother's eye but at the telephone pole in our own (see Matt. 7:3-5). Regular self-evaluation keeps us honest about where we are spiritually and relationally and helps us to eliminate judgmental tendencies. We need to ask ourselves, *Where are my failures? my weaknesses? Where have I blown it?*

Third, when we see our sins and moral failures, God calls us to repent. Humility grows best in the soil of repentance. God calls us to repent wherever and whenever he helps us to see our shortcomings. Repentance is not a onetime deal, but an everyday practice. As we repent of our offenses and shortcomings—and true repentance means that we turn from them and take practical steps to move in the other direction—deep humility results. Go beyond the blatant sins of sexual immorality, Internet pornography, murder, and theft—you can't miss those. Search your heart for symptoms of pride, jealousy, insensitivity, prayerlessness, and neglect.

If God's sons and daughters are ever to come together as one, it's going to take tremendous humility. Those of us from the dominant culture—Gentile Caucasians—must adopt a posture of humility even to be able to hear God's call. We must be willing to hear what might be hard for us to hear, to repent when God shows us our faults, and to humbly commit to continue moving forward when the path grows steep and rocky. At the same time, deep humility is required from those in the communities of color, or any group in the minority. Humble men of God must be willing to stand up and say, "My Gentile brothers, I want to share with you what my burden is like. And I'm here to tell you, I need you." Pastors, you must go this way yourselves before you can lead your men down this necessary path.

Will everyone hear God's call for deep humility? No. Who will? No one can answer that question except the one who hears it. That's why Jesus constantly said, "He who has ears to hear, let him hear." He knew that not everyone would accept his message. Only you can decide whether it's a message you will heed.

THE OBSTACLE OF FEAR

Even those who hear God's call to "come near" to their estranged brothers sometimes shrink back. What keeps them from taking a step of faith to help heal the breach that divides God's church? Sometimes it's ego, and oftentimes it's fear. The two fit together like diabolical scissors to cut up the church. When fear and concern for yourself dominate, blind spots result.

Jesus was *selfless*. He is God, yet he came to earth as a man humbling himself. Jesus was *fearless*. He took mankind's sins to the cross, bearing the burden of all of our mistakes. "Christ in you, the hope of glory" (Col. 1:27). To the extent Jesus emerges in us, we have value. To be spiritually sick is to be selfish and fearful. When we put self first, we are impaired. When we are fearful, we are less able to reflect Christ.

Selfish & Fearful	Reduce freedom.
Selfish & Fearful	Prevent faith.
Selfish & Fearful	Steal your joy.
Selfish & Fearful	Rob you of fruit.
Selfish & Fearful	Limit your witness.
Selfish & Fearful	Compromise authority.
Selfish & Fearful	Divide the church.

Selfish & Fearful	Separate friends.
Selfish & Fearful	Render motives impure.
Selfish & Fearful	Produce offense and defense.
Selfish & Fearful	Hinder prayer.
Selfish & Fearful	Shut down love.
Selfish & Fearful	Carry out the desires of the flesh.
Selfish & Fearful	Oppose the spirit.

The presence of God in a man's life will bring to fruition the healing of selfish and fearful motives that war against the work of the Holy Spirit.

"Come Near to Me"

To God	Fulfills the whole gospel.
To one another	This is a heart condition that will invite our Father's pleasure and presence. (Ps. 16:11: "You will fill me with joy in your presence.")

To fear God is to be fearless with men.

"Let those who fear You turn to me, those who know Your testimonies." (Ps. 119:79, NKJV)

"Now this is the confidence that we have in Him, that if we ask anything according to His will, He hears us. And if we know that He hears us, whatever we ask, we know that we have the petitions that we have asked of Him."
(1 John 5:14-15, NKJV)

"When the enemy shall come in like a flood, the Spirit of the Lord shall lift up a standard against him." (Isa. 59:19, KJV)

For the urban pastor, it might be fear of rejection. No one likes to feel rejected, and if it happens often enough, many decide the high risk outweighs any possible benefit.

For the suburban pastor, it might be fear of the unknown. We fear what we do not understand. And the less contact we have with something, the more we fear it.

Keith Philips, who directs a Christian ministry in Los Angeles, has tried in his corner of the world to address both of those fears. He recruits suburban missionaries and sends them into the inner city. These men and women teach in schools and help to plant churches. We once asked Keith, "Your school is 6 percent African American and 40 percent Hispanic. Why are all the teachers white?"

One of the reasons, he said, is to help heal the divide in the church. Urban pastors can come to know the commitment of suburban men and women to the needs of the city, and suburban believers can come to see the inner city as it truly is, not as Hollywood portrays it. These missionaries don't commute but live in the neighborhood where they minister.

Ultimately, the best way to combat fear is through committed, long-term relationships. Only through such relationships can you learn what you don't know.

When Raleigh pastored the Rock of Our Salvation Free Church in Chicago, he became the only African American, inner-city pastor to join the local urban ministerial association; the rest came from metropolitan Chicago. For five years Raleigh attended the district conference, held at various member churches. One day he said, "Guys, it's time to have a conference at Rock Church."

"I could never bring my people to Rock Church," many replied. "What about their cars? What about their safety?"

Raleigh appealed to the relationship he had established with these men. "Brothers," he said to them, "you have been telling me that you love me; now it's time to show it. We need to have the next meeting at Rock Church. And if you show up without all of your people, then I'll know that you don't really love me."

Raleigh challenged his friends, based on the relationships he had developed—and they all showed up. He welcomed them all to the conference with the greeting, "For five dollars each, I'll return all your hubcaps."

A roar of laughter went up from the audience, signaling a powerful release of tension. How did Raleigh help his friends overcome their fears? By appealing to an existing relationship that had been developing for five years.

Of course, "We have to admit that not all of the fear is invalid," Raleigh cautioned, "'cause the brothers *will* break into your car. When they see white folks come in, dollar signs go up. So I had twelve men patrolling the street. I made sure that we didn't lose any hubcaps."

Still, we can't eliminate all risk. True compassion *chooses* to take risks. It makes sacrifices. People who think they might not be at physical risk when they go into an urban area are naïve. "Let's be honest," Raleigh says, "there are some people who just flat out hate white people. To say that nothing bad is ever going to happen is to fail to understand. Nevertheless, we put our lives on the line for these things; this is the gospel. I feel there is a serious call of God on our lives to go into areas where we may not be safe."

Yet is this easy? Hardly. Sociologists Emerson and Smith write, "Although several evangelicals discuss the personal sacrifice necessary to form friendships across race, their solutions do not require financial or cultural sacrifice. They do not advocate or support changes that might cause extensive discomfort or change their economic and cultural lives. In short, they maintain what is for them the non-costly status quo."[1]

Our situation calls for sacrifice. It calls for us to take risks. And we respond despite our fear. Such determined action takes the kind of courage that only God can supply.

WHAT WORKS?

Relationships work. Not just casual connections, but friendships that knit people together intimately. We need to learn to think about bonds with one another at different levels. This will be addressed in detail in chapter 7, but before we can go further I need to introduce the concept of four levels of relationship.

Virtually all relationships begin by making someone's acquaintance. The next level is achieved when we begin to feel comfortable around our new friend. At the third level we begin to depend on this person, to see him as a friend, to share some significant aspects of our life confidently. But Level Four relationships go far beyond friendship into the uncharted region of intimacy. This intimacy has nothing to do with feelings of sensual attraction. This is about vulnerability, about sharing our most protected feelings of fear, rejection, pain, hope, and faith.

If we are unwilling to move into Level Four relationships with other men, we will never reach a point where we are sharing what really matters to us. There is no substitute for intimacy if we hope to build bridges across the alienation that separates us.

In the past Promise Keepers tried to deal with the issues of racial and Jew-Gentile reconciliation primarily from the standpoint of knowledge. Once people understood the issues, we thought, we could move ahead. So we developed eight biblical principles of reconciliation and held mandatory meetings among our staff. We attacked the problem with knowledge. The result? All our efforts came up short. They didn't take root and germinate.

Today, without neglecting education, we emphasize committed, long-term relationships. Our RID team (reconciliation, inclusivity, and diversity) operates from the basis of relationship, not merely knowledge. We have to be in relationship with one another. We have to move toward the level of intimacy. We've been at this for eleven years, and the only thing we've found that truly works is relationships. Everything else has a short life.

If our board of directors is working toward intimacy; if our executive cabinet is working toward intimacy; if every director of every team is working toward intimacy—then we can "come near" to one another in our corner of the world.

Of course, that takes dogged persistence and time. A short time ago we invited a consultant to do an analysis and give some recommendations regarding proposed changes in Promise Keepers's ministry of reconciliation. He concluded that different visions for the ministry existed within our organization. Even at the top leadership levels, differing views and perspectives existed regarding what was and what ought to be. Without agreement over the vision, of course, we were bound to have problems. Since then we have addressed many of those difficulties and have reduced the problems, but even today we must work to make sure that everyone within the ministry shares a common vision.

I believe that pastors must create relationships moving toward intimacy among members of their staff, elders, deacons, program leaders, and beyond. Level Four relationships facilitate unity in vision, purpose, and ministry. Intimacy is critical in developing the spiritual lives of men. Men need to be reminded of the relationships Jesus had with his twelve disciples. And remember this: God says that nothing is impossible for those who are in one accord (see Ecc. 4:12).

KEEP ON MAKING ROOM

Ultimately, we have to keep on making room in our hearts for one another, despite our failures, despite our lack of shared vision, despite our screwups and mistakes. To make room in my own heart, I begin by praying every day for specific individuals and groups. I may struggle with them, or they may struggle with me. In my daily prayers, I pray that God will bless them, their ministry, and their family. I ask God to help me make room in my heart for them. This practice has softened me and deepened my humility.

The dominant culture of this country has never suffered much from a lack of resources and all the evils that accompany such a lack. It's for that reason that members of the dominant culture must make *more* room when it comes to inclusivity and diversity. The individual from the dominant culture must be willing to say, regarding his ethnic brother, "He's going to say some things that I'm not going to understand. And he's going to say some other things that will sting. But rather than feel offended and close my heart, I have to develop a capacity to understand what he's saying and to consider how I can be part of the solution. I have to make more room in my heart."

Where can we find the motivation for doing this? We remind ourselves that the divide between urban and suburban continues to grow wider each day, even though most in the majority culture do not see it. The communities of color, however, see the *growing divide* both clearly and almost unanimously. As Christians who love the Lord Jesus, we have no option but to make more room in our heart.

Part of that "more room" involves sacrifice. We cannot begin to close such a wide division without sacrifice, without intentionally moving out of our comfort zones in order to facilitate the relationship. Some things will have to change. If healing is our goal, then comfort cannot be our means. And when cultures collide, discomfort normally occurs.

Let me give a simple example of how differences in culture can cause hurts and prompt us to close up emotionally. The Hispanic community typically doesn't pay as much attention to timetables and schedules as does the Anglo community. You can invite a Latino to an event and he'll say, "I'll be there." And then he doesn't come. And when you ask him about it, he'll say, "Well, in my culture, we don't always say yes or no."

Now, when something like that happens, you have a choice. Will you make room in your heart? Or will you be offended and jettison the relationship?

I'm very much a part of the Anglo world of schedules and being on time. If my friends from the suburban churches think we're going to meet at 11 A.M., and my friends from the urban churches don't arrive until 11:45 A.M., we already have a problem. The Anglos will say, "They don't respect us; they don't honor us. We're trying to make a relationship here, and they don't even have enough respect to come on time." Meanwhile, the ethnic brothers will say, "Why should we always have to conform to their culture? Why can't they understand and accept ours?"

Both sides have to make room in their hearts for the other—to be willing to forgive, to be forgiven, and to change. And yet it might also help to make some ground rules to help things progress more smoothly.

I'll never forget what Michigan football coach Bo Schembechler did one afternoon. Several minutes after a scheduled meeting had begun, one of his players snuck in the back door and slipped into the auditorium where more than one hundred players already had gathered. Bo saw the kid and shouted, "Smith! Stand up!"

So Smith stood up. "What you're telling me," Bo said, "is that your time is more important than all of our time. You're telling me that I'm supposed to hold everybody here until you get here—is that right, Smith? That's not how we do things here. Do you understand me, Son? Now, get out of here. And if you ever come late again, you ain't on this team."

Smith never came late again. Neither did anybody else.

The interesting thing is that half of the guys in the room came from cultures that don't especially value timeliness. Maybe the kids were used to getting to church half an hour late. But all of a sudden, a ground rule had been established, and that changed everything.

Of course, I'm not recommending that pastors and other church leaders adopt Bo's method. But I am suggesting that we capture the principle: Clear ground rules pave the way for success. Establishing mutually acceptable ground rules helps to head off many of the problems in cross-cultural exchanges.

Still, we have to count on some rough roads. To deal with them, we have to learn to make room in our hearts. Humility and resolve go a long way toward achieving the success we crave. We have to keep getting up and getting back into the game. We have to put everything on the table and swallow hard.

Without a determination to resolve conflict, we cannot achieve any great measure of success. Into every relationship, conflict will come. The question is, will we make room in our hearts for the one who has wounded or injured us? When we remain committed to the individuals, we find the strength and will to confront and resolve our conflicts so that our relationships can continue to develop.

HE WALKED SLOWLY

Is it easy to make room in our heart? Not always. Our flesh gets in the way and urges us to choose what's comfortable, what's familiar, what's easy, what's quick. Yet if we are to delight God's heart by coming together as his sons, we have no choice but to make room in our hearts for one another.

And it will take time—probably much longer than any of us knows. There are no instant answers, no single solutions. It will take time. And yet I remember that Jesus walked slowly to the Cross.

That's the only way this thing will ever work.

chapter four GOOD
DEFENSE, POOR OFFENSE

The best football teams always field strong squads on both sides of the ball. Even an exceptional defensive club has to develop an effective offense.

Want proof? Look to the past few years in the National Football League. We've seen a number of NFL clubs with fine defensive squads that had real trouble advancing in the playoffs. Why? They just couldn't score.

While outstanding teams might specialize in offense or defense, they all manage to achieve a good balance. Even the '84 Chicago Bears, widely considered one of the best defensive teams in history, had a solid offense that could effectively put points on the board. The team averaged a little over 28 points in the regular season, 29 in the playoffs. While it boasted such defensive stars as Mike Singletary and

William "the Refrigerator" Perry, it also fielded Jim McMahon and the legendary Walter Payton on offense.

All great teams manage to field strong squads on both offense and defense. Lopsided teams rarely achieve significant success, and they never sustain whatever success they do attain. I believe this principle holds true for any team, whether in athletics, business, or religion.

And that's why this concept, applied to the contemporary church, gives me cause for grave concern.

A RADICAL IMBALANCE

When I look at the American church today, there appears to be a radical imbalance between offense and defense. We have a good defense—week in and week out, evangelical churches do a solid job of preaching righteousness. They proclaim clearly how individuals can get right with God and how they can develop a personal relationship with a loving heavenly Father who wants to help them live in purity. That's our defense in this analogy, and we field a consistently strong one.

But our offense? That's another story.

By offense, I mean doing justice in the way the Bible mandates. When the church fails to mount a public, outward thrust of mercy and compassion, it loses all kinds of opportunities to visibly demonstrate the power and relevancy of the gospel.

I believe that if we could more effectively teach justice and bring it out of our people, we would significantly upgrade our offense—and by so doing, we would win the lost in far greater numbers. If we in the church really did *justice* today, we would turn our culture upside down for Jesus Christ. We need the high-powered offense of justice to make headway in a world deeply suspicious of religious phonies.

Not everyone, of course, believes this. Many Christians assume that the growing problems of our society and the church result from a shortage of personal righteousness. They take it for granted that if we could get larger numbers of people to repent, to fall to their knees and submit to the lordship of Christ, then God would lift up our nation.

While I do not deny that all of us need to continually get down on our knees in genuine repentance, I want to suggest that most of our problems have a different source. We suffer less from a shortage of righteousness than from a scarcity of justice. The bald fact is that the church at large in America is not doing justice. Why not?

I blame a blind spot.

A LOOK AT THE SPLIT

Our failure to do justice arises not from an orchestrated or intentional omission but from blocked vision. The way I see it, while the suburban church focuses on issues of righteousness, the urban church, by necessity, concentrates on problems of justice.

This perspective helps to explain the sharp line of division between Democrats and Republicans. White, conservative Christians tend to vote Republican, while people of color overwhelmingly tend to favor Democratic candidates. We ought to ask ourselves, why did *92 percent* of people of color vote for Al Gore in the last presidential election, rather than for George Bush? This fact greatly puzzles many suburban Christians because Bush has made no secret of his personal faith in Jesus Christ. They wonder, *How could so many urban believers vote for a man who champions abortion? What's wrong with them?*

Meanwhile, many urban Christians question the reality of the faith of their suburban counterparts. They wonder, *What Bible are you reading? How could you vote for a man who favors big business over the poor?*

I think both groups suffer from their own blind spots. Consider the issue of abortion. Many urban believers are blinded to a depth of concern for the unborn because they feel overwhelmed with concern over the already-born poor who are desperately seeking to survive in single-parent homes. Meanwhile, suburban believers who do not regularly face issues of poverty or justice focus on the plight of the unborn, with no conscious awareness of how inner-city believers struggle for survival.

If the church could recognize its blind spots, come together, and speak as one, I believe that we could more effectively minister both to the unborn and the already born. Dr. James Dobson of Focus on the Family has led the fight against abortion—a plague that has taken more than forty million American lives—and yet he often feels as though he stands alone. What would happen if a united church championed both righteousness and justice? What would happen if we chose both, and not one or the other?

The Bible never separates righteousness from justice. It never points us to the two issues and says, "Choose one or the other." It assumes that genuine righteousness in the heart will lead to tangible justice in the community.

Here is an area where Messianic Jewish believers shine with the light of God, simultaneously pursuing and persevering in personal righteousness—the way a disciple of Messiah should live—while practicing justice and compassion in their dealings with others. A community that adopts a lifestyle of justice and mercy with their neighbors, and that exercises personal discipline in prayer and Bible study, attracts seekers. People want to learn more about this Messiah and his loving ways.

Listen to the Lord as he cries out through Isaiah: "Is this the kind of fast I have chosen, only a day for a man to humble himself? Is it only for bowing one's head like a reed and for lying on sackcloth and ashes? Is that what you call a fast, a day acceptable to the Lord?" (Isa. 58:5). All of those things—humbling oneself, praying, prostrating oneself, seeking the Lord—come out of personal righteousness and a man's standing before God. Yet they are not enough. The Lord says that he expects a genuine relationship with him to inevitably reach out into the public arena:

> *Is not this the kind of fasting I have chosen: to loose the chains of injustice and untie the cords of the yoke, to set the oppressed free and break every yoke? Is it not to share your food with the hungry and to provide the poor wanderer with shelter—when you see the naked, to clothe him, and not to turn away from your own flesh and blood? (Isa. 58:6-7)*

When our personal righteousness motivates us to public acts of justice, notice what happens: "Then your light will break forth like the dawn, and your healing will quickly appear; then your righteousness will go before you, and the glory of the Lord will be your rear guard. Then you will call, and the Lord will answer; you will cry for help, and he will say: Here am I" (Isa. 58:8-9).

Jesus always paired concern for personal righteousness with a commitment to public justice. When the imprisoned John the Baptist wondered whether Jesus could really be the Messiah, our Lord didn't respond merely with a description of his personal holiness and calling. Instead he told John's disciples, "Go back and report to John what you hear and see: The blind receive sight, the lame walk, those who have leprosy are cured, the deaf hear, the dead are raised, and the good news is preached to the poor" (Matt. 11:5-6). Anyone can *claim* to be holy and right with God; it's their *behavior* that demonstrates the truth or falsity of their claim.

Scripture teaches believers to champion both justice and righteousness, equally and at the same time. And yet our blind spots often prevent us even from seeing one or the other.

E. K. Bailey, an African American pastor of a church in Dallas, Texas, has worked hard to build relationships across racial lines. He notices a fundamental difference between black and white perspectives. "African Americans lean toward a social emphasis; the white churches lean toward the evangelical, especially in the South," he said. "For some reason, we have not been able to get those two to work in concert."[1]

What keeps us separated? I believe it's a blind spot.

WHY THE SPLIT?

Because the suburban church does not generally face issues of justice in order to survive, it preaches righteousness; in most cases, justice doesn't become a big part of its ministry. Suburban pastors tend to ask themselves, "What can I tell my people to help them live a more righteous life?" They focus on Bible knowledge and personal devotion more than on meeting acute human need.

On the other hand, the urban church cannot survive without concentrating on justice. While it, too, preaches personal righteousness, its people live in the midst of deplorable conditions that demand change. Most suburban churchgoers have little idea of the enormous challenges facing their fellow believers in the city.

Raleigh Washington, who is, you'll recall, my best friend at Promise Keepers, used to pastor the Rock of Our Salvation Free Church in Chicago, Illinois. A full 60 percent of his members were single moms on welfare, most on fixed incomes. When someone in his church died, he often had to scramble to find ways to scrape together enough money just to bury the deceased. And that's just one illustration of the challenges he faced.

"We are growing a fatherless society in America," Raleigh said. "Three out of ten Anglo kids wake up every morning without a father, while the ratio is five out of ten for Hispanic and Native American children. But in the urban inner city, *nine out of ten* African American kids wake up with no father in the home. The urban church has a tremendous need for mentors. The issues of justice are everywhere."

So far we've suggested that the suburban church tends to focus on righteousness, while the urban church focuses on justice. Why? "Necessity" provides part of the answer. History may supply another reason.

THE INFLUENCE OF THEOLOGICAL HISTORY

Not long ago I spoke on the phone with Jack Hayford, founding pastor of the Church on the Way in Van Nuys, California. Jack believes that the forces of theological history have played a large role in the unbiblical separation of righteousness from justice. After our conversation he sent me a fax to clarify his thinking.

"The primary problem in getting white evangelicals to perceive social justice and meeting human economic and social need as a 'righteousness' issue can be traced to the impact of a particular theological mind-set," he wrote. "That mind-set flows out of the Reformation era in which the primary issue was the individual's relationship with God."

Jack contends that a focus on "me" and "my relationship with God"—and a concern to help others "get right with God through a salvation attained by grace through faith"—focused the church's attention on the private standing of an individual before the Lord, with a special emphasis on justification.

"Anything that proposes there are other features of 'righteousness' is suspected as 'works,'" he writes, "and is either rejected out of hand, or neglected as relatively unimportant." When we insist that true righteousness requires action, such as attempts at ethnic reconciliation or serving urban need and human brokenness in our cities, "we are easily dispensed with as preoccupied with 'works.' These works may be acknowledged as 'nice,' 'good,' or 'gracious,' but they still have little to do with 'the righteousness of God' and are not necessary in order to fulfill 'righteousness.'"

Jack emphasizes that most believers who operate according to this mind-set *don't realize they think that way*. They are *structured* to think this way by two things: (1) the flow of theological history in the church, which confines 'righteousness' to the soul's 'justification'; and (2) the fact that the European–White American church community has historically NOT suffered economic need—certainly not as the Black or Hispanic or Native American. In other words, *ideologically* they are 'theologized' to overlook social justice as 'righteousness,' and *pragmatically* they are insulated from sensitivity to the need for social justice."

Jack likens the current situation to the days before the Civil War, when many Christians attempted to justify their practice of slavery: "While American whites caused black exploitation via slavery (and gave biblical excuses for doing so), they now tend to continue by blindly excusing themselves from accepting a larger responsibility in addressing urban need. No one consciously reasons this way, but the drift of history has produced the attitude: *The needs of the city are worthy of attention, but they really aren't my job. Anyway, they have nothing to do with anything ultimate. And besides, my heart's right with God. Everything's fine as long as I feel okay about God and me.*

"In short," he writes, "if it doesn't have to do with me and God, it doesn't ultimately make any difference."

While Jack admits his perspective may sound "a little stark," I think Jack may be on to something. He also believes that such an understanding helps to explain the peculiar fact that while most suburban churches have little to do with their urban counterparts, they do send vast amounts of money overseas.

"Curiously," he writes, "Euro-American Christians *will* rally for foreign missions and human need there, but that is seen as worthy because 'we're doing this for souls.' In other words, *simply reaching with good works to rectify circumstances in which people need care* is not, in and of itself, deemed a sufficient reason to invest."[2]

I believe Jack's analysis to be right on target. Suburban Christians don't consciously shut the inner city out of their hearts; they simply have been conditioned not to see the need. They suffer from a blind spot—a blind spot made more acute, I think, by another more recent historical episode.

AN OLD CONTROVERSY LIVES ON

At the beginning of the last century, an impressive list of conservative Christian scholars undertook the task of writing, publishing, and distributing a twelve-volume series on the essentials of the Christian faith that they called *The Fundamentals.* They designed the series to combat a rising liberal theology that in essence denied the supernatural and attacked the integrity of the Bible. Those in the liberal camp came to be known as "modernists," while members of the conservative camp got the label "fundamentalists."

The conflict between the two groups quickly became bitter and heated, so much so that anything the one group supported, the other group condemned. Because the modernists championed "the social gospel"—that is, addressing the material and educational needs of the poor and disenfranchised but emphatically without the spiritual component of salvation by grace through faith in a risen Christ—most fundamentalists began to see any kind of social outreach as a compromise of the gospel.

Although the original modernist/fundamentalist controversy has long since faded, many of its effects remain. Most suburban evangelical groups trace their theological roots back to the fundamentalists of the last century and thus continue to harbor deep suspicions of anything that looks like "the social gospel."

While we owe a great debt to our theological forebears for safeguarding, articulating, and defending "the faith that was once for all entrusted to the saints" (Jude 1:3), it is past time that we rediscovered the justice component of that faith. We must ask ourselves, how can we neglect what God himself so passionately advocates?

GOD'S PLEASURE IN JUSTICE

In scores of passages throughout the Bible, God declares his delight in both righteousness and justice. Time after time, Scripture pairs the very traits that we too often separate. Consider some telling testimony from the book of Psalms. King David tells us, "For the Lord is righteous, he loves justice" (Ps. 11:7).

Furthermore, since "The Lord loves righteousness and justice" (Ps. 33:5), David tells God, "Your righteousness is like the mighty mountains, your justice like the great deep" (Ps. 36:6). Both lovely traits so characterize God's nature that the psalmist tells him, "Righteousness and justice are the foundation of your throne" (Ps. 89:14). Therefore it comes as no surprise that God "will judge the world in righteousness; he will govern the peoples with justice" (Ps. 9:8).

For good reason, many believers name Jeremiah 9:23-24 as their favorite verse. "This is what the Lord says," the prophet declares: "'Let not the wise man boast of his wisdom or the strong man boast of his strength or the rich man boast of his riches, but let him who boasts boast about this: that he understands and knows me, that I am the Lord, who exercises kindness, justice and righteousness on earth, for in these I delight,' declares the Lord." The word translated *kindness* is the Hebrew term *hesed*, which refers to the Lord's covenant love and is sometimes rendered loving-kindness. The authors of the *Theological Wordbook of the Old Testament* say that *hesed* "is a kind of love, including mercy . . . when the object is in a pitiful state. It often takes verbs of action, 'do,' 'keep,' and so refers to acts of love as well as to the attribute. The word 'lovingkindness' of the KJV is archaic, but not far from the fullness of the meaning of the word."[3]

God advises us not to glory in our mental capabilities, for they are temporary. He counsels us not to hang our hat on our strength, for it's as nothing compared to him. He warns us not to exult in our wealth, because it can soon vanish. If we boast in anything, it ought to be that we understand who he really is. And who is he? He is a God who *delights* in justice and righteousness. That is where we find God's pleasure.

So doesn't it make sense that he would require of us the very things that delight his heart? And what does God require of us? Micah makes it explicit: "To act justly and to love mercy and to walk humbly with your God" (Mic. 6:8).

God is saying to us, "Do you really know and understand me? Then you know that I delight in justice—and that I require you to reflect my character and to delight in justice by doing justice yourself. Get to know those in my family who need your help! The more you get to know them, the more you can become part of the solution. The more you understand their needs— needs that do not escape my attention—the more you will see how you can do justice in their lives."

Just before Jesus ascended into heaven, he took Peter aside to officially restore the chastened apostle to the gospel ministry. As Peter had denied the Lord three times before the Crucifixion, so after the Resurrection the Lord three times asked Peter, "Do you love me?" Each time, the burly fisherman replied in the affirmative. And how did Jesus respond? "Feed my lambs," he told Peter. "Take care of my sheep. . . . Feed my sheep" (John 21:15-17). The words he so carefully chose demonstrate our Lord's intense concern for the brotherhood of believers. In the most powerful yet tender way imaginable, Jesus expressed to Peter his desire that Christian leaders show true compassion and justice to his beloved sheep. Peter showed that he "got" the lesson when he wrote in 1 Peter 2:17, "Love the brotherhood."

The fact is, our Lord could hardly conceive of a true believer who would consciously turn his back on a brother in need. So closely did he associate personal righteousness with public justice that he insisted the absence of one indicated the nonexistence of the other. On the day he returns to earth, he said, he will "separate the people one from another as a shepherd separates the sheep from the goats" (Matt. 25:32). To the sheep he will say, "Come, you who are blessed by my Father; take your inheritance, the kingdom prepared for you since the creation of the world. For I was hungry and you gave me something to eat, I was thirsty and you gave me something to drink, I was a stranger and you invited me in, I needed clothes and you clothed me, I was sick and you looked after me, I was in prison and you came to visit me" (Matt. 25:34-36).

The sheep—"the righteous"—will protest, "Lord, when did we see you hungry and feed you, or thirsty and give you something to drink? When did we see you a stranger and invite you in, or needing clothes and clothe you? When did we see you sick or in prison and go to visit you?" Then the Lord will reply, "I tell you the truth, whatever you did for one of the least of these brothers of mine, you did for me" (Matt. 25:37-40).

The goats, on the other hand—the "cursed"—will be sent into "the eternal fire prepared for the devil and his angels." Why? Because they did *not* do the same acts of justice performed by the righteous (see 25:41-45).

When I pointed out this text to a pastor friend of mine, he replied with a start, "I never saw this before. I always saw that as a passage related to Israel. But I see now I was wrong."

My friend had not recognized this text as a mandate to the church. He hadn't seen it as a driving application for the here-and-now—and therefore he had unwittingly neglected the work Jesus had called him to do.

Jesus often emphasized this message of justice. When a teacher of the Law asked the Lord to name the greatest commandment, the Master replied, "The most important one . . . is this: 'Hear, O Israel, the Lord our God, the Lord is one. Love the Lord your God with all your heart and with all your soul and with all your mind and with all your strength.' The second is this:

'Love your neighbor as yourself.' There is no commandment greater than these" (Mark 12:29-31).

The man had asked Jesus to name one commandment, and Jesus gave him two. Or did he? It's true that he quoted two separate commandments from the Old Testament (Deut. 6:4-5 and Lev. 19:18, respectively), but then he said something very curious. "There is no commandment [singular] greater than these [plural]," he declared. Jesus apparently saw these two commandments as different sides of the same coin. And that explains a number of important passages from the New Testament.

TRUE RELIGION

The book of James puts shoe leather to the New Testament's theology of grace. "Religion that God our Father accepts as pure and faultless is this: to look after orphans and widows in their distress and to keep oneself from being polluted by the world" (James 1:27).

Here again we see righteousness and justice paired up. To keep oneself unspotted from the world is the epitome of righteousness. James tells us that we need to be among the unconverted but separate from them. We need to be in them but not of them. They need to see in us the righteousness that God gives to us. But "religion that God our Father accepts" can't stop with righteousness. What good would that be? In fact, how can we be unspotted and righteous and above reproach if we're not giving a social expression to the gospel? We can't. Therefore James tells us to live out our righteousness by looking after "orphans and widows in their distress." Any religion that fails to do that, God cannot accept.

True religion is to minister to those who can't return the favor. We need the poor for that very reason. We need them in order to "do" true religion. We need them if we are to do justice and thereby fulfill what God has commissioned us to do. This is the gospel as it is socially expressed, not the social gospel.

Think of the story of the Good Samaritan (see Luke 10:30-37). Jesus told this parable to a lawyer who clearly did not like the idea that love for God required an ensuing love for one's "neighbor." So the man demanded, "And who is my neighbor?" Jesus' answer: anyone in need within range of your eyes.

Now if the Lord said that for an individual, he also said it for the church. If a prosperous church looks across town and sees another church half dead, how can it do less than the Samaritan did for the Jew? The Samaritan in Jesus' story gave the beaten man some medicine, supplied him with hospitality, and arranged for transportation. The Living Bible says, "He nursed him through the night" (v. 34). The Samaritan left several needed resources with the injured man and promised to return so that he might check up on the man's welfare—and Jesus told the lawyer, "Go and do likewise" (v. 37).

What a picture for us in the church! If a Samaritan could act so neighborly toward a stranger from an enemy culture, shouldn't one part of God's family be able to reach out a neighborly hand to another part of God's family?

God certainly seems to think so. "For anyone who does not love his brother, whom he has seen," says the apostle John, "cannot love God, whom he has not seen" (1 John 4:20). Not only so, but, "If anyone has material possessions and sees his brother in need but has no pity on him, how can the love of God be in him? Dear children, let us not love with words or tongue but with actions and in truth" (1 John 3:17-18).

In the Bible, the words *righteous* and *just* are so closely related that often the two terms can be substituted for one another. Consider 1 John 1:9. The New International Version offers the translation, "If we confess our sins, he is faithful and *just*," while the New American Standard Bible renders the verse, "If we confess our sins, He is faithful and *righteous*" (italics added for emphasis).

James, too, reminds us of the connection between righteousness and justice. In his own commentary on the theme of the Good Samaritan, he asks,

> *What good is it, my brothers, if a man claims to have faith but has no deeds? Can such faith save him? Suppose a brother or sister is without clothes and daily food. If one of you says to him, "Go, I wish you well; keep warm and well fed," but does nothing about his physical needs, what good is it? In the same way, faith by itself, if it is not accompanied by action, is dead. But someone will say, "You have faith; I have deeds." Show me your faith without deeds, and I will show you my faith by what I do. (James 2:14-18)*

A Good Samaritan church does not choose between faith and deeds, any more than it chooses between righteousness and justice. It shows its faith by what it does. It reflects God's character by championing both righteousness and justice.

A THEOLOGIAN WEIGHS IN

We asked Gordon R. Lewis, senior professor of systematic theology and Christian philosophy at Denver Seminary and our beloved resident theologian here at Promise Keepers, to help us understand whether righteousness and justice can be biblically separated from one another. "After examining many passages on God's righteousness in Himself and His justice or fairness in dealing with others," he writes, "it is emphatic that in God, righteousness and justice are inseparable."

Furthermore, he writes, "After examining many passages on God's people, it is equally emphatic that believers *ought* to be both righteous in themselves and just in their relationships with others. . . . Experientially, it is difficult to see how the relation of a believer to God could be righteous when he is not also fair in his dealings with his brothers and neighbors."

Biblically speaking, then, a man who has graciously received a righteous standing before God through faith in Jesus Christ *ought* to express his personal righteousness through works of public justice. And if he doesn't? In that case, the Bible leaves an arrow sticking in his conscience: "How can the love of God be in him?" (1 John 3:17).

Take special note of Dr. Lewis's final two questions: "If we are not righteous in ourselves before God, is it not unlikely that we will be just in our dealings with humans? If we are not fair in our treatment of others, are we right before God?"[4]

Those are good questions. How would you answer them?

JUSTICE AS A LIFESTYLE

For the last several years Promise Keepers has stood strong in the area of racial reconciliation. We've shouted the message for so long and so hard that whenever we repeat it, almost immediately we begin to get "pushed back."

"We understand it, we've done a few things toward it, and that should be it," comes the reply. "We have a homeless ministry and a benevolent fund, so we've covered our bases."

But it's a whole lot more than that. God wants "doing justice" to become a lifestyle, an integral part of everything we do. If we try it as a side activity, it soon becomes a sideshow. Justice must become a part of our life, even as righteousness has become a part of our life.

And how can justice become a part of our life? Realistically, we have found that the only way it happens is through long-term, committed relationships between men of differing cultures. Friendships tend to move through four levels, from acquaintance to intimacy. In chapter 6 we will argue that what we call "Level Four" relationships—committed friendships that work to achieve a deep, transparent, and vulnerable level of nonsexual intimacy—are the key to building the momentum required for justice to flourish. Jesus and John, for example, had a "Level Four" friendship. Without a commitment to developing such deep relationships, justice is likely to remain little more than a great idea.

It's also important to realize that we don't do justice because we have to; we do justice because we get to. We do justice out of the same compassion that drove Jesus to minister to the hurting multitudes.

What is compassion? Most definitions come back to the ideas of "sympathy" and "pity." But compassion encompasses much more than a strong emotion. Compassion moves from sympathy or pity to some kind of remedial action. Compassion agitates something within your soul that compels you to respond. It's one thing to look at someone with pity; it's another to feel so stirred within your heart that you just *have* to do something. You simply can't leave and walk away. You feel compelled to take action, to respond, to bring about some kind of positive change.

The intriguing thing is, when you respond with that kind of hands-on compassion, others see it—and wonder what's going on.

EXPLOSIVE EVANGELISM

Why does today's church struggle so mightily? Why are only one percent of churches growing? Why are such large numbers of young people not accepting Christ? Why do 80 percent of young adults reared in the church abandon the church after they turn eighteen?

I say it's a relevancy issue. The church has lost much of its potency because observers do not see its relevance to society's growing problems. Young people may think like this: *If the "power of God in Christ" cannot even bring together the estranged members of the urban and suburban church, then why bother with the church at all?*

It's not enough to have a good defense; it's not enough to preach righteousness alone. To get back into title contention, to regain our winning ways, we have to rebuild our offense. We must relearn how to do justice.

In a world that many have called both "post-Christian" and "postmodern," the church has to show what a difference the gospel can make in the here and now. We cannot merely speak of the peace we feel inside because of the righteousness Jesus Christ has imparted to us. We must be able to show the world that true faith—true religion—habitually lends a helping hand to those in need. Only then will large numbers of men and women from the general culture begin to say, "Man, they got it right! They really seem to love each other. I wonder if they have room for me?"

I'm not guessing about this. Both Scripture and experience prove it. Jesus promised, "By this *all men will know that you are my disciples,* if you love one another" (John 13:35, emphasis added). Near the end of his earthly ministry, our Lord prayed to his Father about his disciples, "May they be brought to complete unity *to let the world know that you sent me and have loved them* even as you have loved me" (John 17:23, emphasis added).

In the early church, the disciples not only "devoted themselves to the apostles' teaching and to the fellowship, to the breaking of bread and to prayer" but also "gave to anyone as he had need." And the result? Luke writes, "The Lord added to their number daily those who were being saved" (Acts 2:42-47).

A little later, an issue of injustice caused a rift in the church. One part of the church complained against another part "because their widows were being overlooked in the daily distribution of food" (Acts 6:1). So what did the apostles do? Without sacrificing any emphasis on righteousness, they directed gifted men to redress the grievance and do justice. The result? "The number of disciples in Jerusalem increased rapidly, and a large number of priests became obedient to the faith" (Acts 6:7).

God never meant for righteousness and justice to exist separately. When both work together as in Acts, as God intended, when both believing Jews and Gentiles are one, explosive evangelism results.

Doing justice, without sacrificing righteousness, is a potent way to bring life to a congregation that seems largely comatose.

Doing justice, without sacrificing righteousness, is an effective way to keep our children passionate about following Jesus.

Doing justice, without sacrificing righteousness, is the best way to heal the growing divide in the American church.

I believe our pews are full of guys who have made authentic decisions for Jesus Christ. They're genuinely converted and they're sitting out there—but they're not boiling over for God. If someone ever lit their fuse, however, watch out! You'd see the water bubble and steam.

Do you know what's holding most of these guys back? They've been on the defensive side of the ball so long that they're not even sure what a good offense looks like. Most guys, however, like to score points. Watch the face of a defensive lineman who gets to score a touchdown. He feels alive!

Imagine what would happen if the guys in our churches ever learned to do justice. Imagine what would happen if they got a taste of a powerful offense. I guarantee they would come alive. It's in giving that you receive (Acts 20:35). If the men in our churches were ever challenged to take their free time and give it away for the cause of Christ, they would discover a joy they'd never known. They would enter a level of spirituality that they never thought possible.

That's what a good offense can do for you. And that's exactly what we need.

chapter five

COME NEAR TO ME

Representatives of Promise Keepers recently met with the pastor of a very large suburban church. We wanted to talk about how his congregation might be able to partner with struggling urban churches in his area. We didn't expect his response.

"I'm sorry," the pastor said, "but I don't have time to meet with people of color. Do you know why? All they want is money. I'm sorry to be so crass, but that's just the way I feel. And I don't *want* to be a part of any other group. I'm happy with what I'm doing."

End of meeting.

The man's breathtakingly blunt comments floored us—but maybe they shouldn't have. This man obviously operates from a bad experience or from a negative personal report. He really thinks that all urban churches want money, and

money alone, from their wealthier brothers in the suburbs. He suffers from a blind spot—and he's not the only one.

Inner-city pastors often operate under an equally damaging blind spot. "All they're concerned about are their programs and their buildings," we hear them say of their suburban counterparts. "They have all the money they need; they don't care about us. They're arrogant, overfed, and unconcerned."

Perhaps blind spots keep suburban and inner-city pastors from seeing the need to include Messianic Jewish congregations and their pastors in their thinking. Many Messianic pastors and their congregations have never been invited to celebrate an Easter sunrise service with a number of other congregations. How many clergy luncheons have overlooked these pastors? Is it unreasonable for Messianic Jewish Christians to hope that believers from across the spectrum would want to include them in their plans, prayers, and patronage?

From my heart, I believe we make such hurtful statements because we don't know what we don't know. Blind spots keep us apart. If we ever tried hard to discover what we don't know about one another, the church would change drastically.

I believe the Father heart of God is waiting for the members of his church to hear one another, understand one another, and work closely with one another for his glory and their benefit. I believe the Lord wants to revive his church. More than anything, I think the Lord is saying to us, "I want my sons to come together."

WHEN MISUNDERSTANDINGS MULTIPLY

Blind spots can afflict us all. And when they do, misunderstandings multiply.

Consider just a few of these damaging misconceptions. Many members of the urban community doubt that those in the suburban community really care about their plight. They believe that in their fight for ministry, they have been left wounded and half naked on the side of the road, much like the injured man in Jesus' parable of the Good Samaritan. They have greater needs than available resources, and it seems to them that the suburban church members, much like the priest and the Levite in Jesus' parable, walk by on the other side of the road.

Because of these misunderstandings, the urban pastor often does not trust the concerned suburban pastor who says to him, "What can I do?" He doesn't accept the genuine heart of so many suburban pastors who legitimately want to respond. Why not? He's been burned before, and he has no intention of getting burned again.

Several years ago an Anglo friend of mine who works in the Christian publishing industry made this discovery for himself. His boss was concerned that the inner-city church lacked Christian literature geared to its needs, so he sent my friend on a nationwide tour of some leading urban ministries to find out how the need might be addressed. One question came up repeatedly: "Are you in this for the long haul, or is this just another project that will get dropped if it doesn't produce results quickly enough?"

My friend didn't quite know how to respond. He told these leaders that he considered his boss's concern genuine, but that he couldn't make any promises. "I can't guarantee what my company will do," he said, "but isn't it worth the risk?"

Most of these leaders agreed that it was, joined an advisory board, made a trip to the publishing company—and several months later saw their efforts go up in smoke. The publishing company ran into a dry sales period, and the new initiative never got off the ground. I suspect that many of these men and women returned to their homes and ministries thinking, *Just one more example of the suburban church walking by on the other side of the road.*

But could it be that the suburban church walks by because it honestly doesn't see the need? From its vantage point, no bleeding man lies beaten and bruised on the side of the road. What it sees is a culture it can't understand. The suburban church doesn't have a bad heart; it just hasn't grasped the real need. Besides, it can name example after example where it tried to minister side by side with urban believers—note the incident above—but for some reason, things never worked out. So it decides to go it alone in ministry. If it could begin to get a burden for the plight of the urban church, however, its heart for the poor would soon begin to enlarge. It would become increasingly sensitive to needs it once couldn't see.

What fuels our misperceptions? Why do we keep missing each other? I think much of it comes down to a lack of full and open communication. Most men and women of color have never told their Anglo counterparts the full burden of pain that they bear. They have never felt "safe" enough to describe their wounds. So they keep quiet—and so both churches keep missing one another, like trains passing in the night.

Again, the key to reducing and eliminating such hurtful misperceptions is to develop cross-cultural relationships that reach Level Four. When an Anglo leader and a leader of color set out to establish a Level Four friendship, a deeply wounded man will reveal his innermost pain. And it's hard for us to misperceive what we receive firsthand.

THE PAIN THAT SILENCES

Most of my Anglo friends have a hard time understanding why the African American community seemed to celebrate so wildly over the 2002 Oscar wins by Halle Berry (best actress) and Denzel Washington (best actor). "What's the big deal?" they asked. "Why all the fuss?"

What's the big deal? I'll tell you. Despite many hard-won gains in civil rights over the past forty years, most people of color in America still feel "left out" of the American dream. They think that a condescending, dominant culture looks for ways to say, "You need me, but I don't need you."

When Halle Berry wept uncontrollably after receiving her Oscar, she expressed the hope that maybe—just maybe—the door of opportunity had at last swung open for all people of color. The fact is, the minority cultures in this nation are hurting, largely because they're made to feel irrelevant and unimportant.

Level Four relationships have given me empathy for all minorities. I may not understand specifics, but my close friends of color have engendered in me a sensitivity for all minorities.

"The wounding of a person of color is deep," says Ray Vialpando, director with U.S. ministries at Promise Keepers. "Whether that wound is caused intentionally or unintentionally, the pain is the same. If you don't know how to wield the sword, you can hurt people all over the place and not even be aware of it."

Messianic Jewish Christians have, for about seventeen centuries, been left out in the cold by their Gentile brethren. Can we even begin to imagine the kind of bitter discouragement, or the painful feelings of betrayal, they must overcome to be willing to become vulnerable and intimate with Gentile believers?

This disconnect between speaker and listener may not even involve the specifics of an offense or pain. It may not get that far. To be ignored can be even more painful than someone not fully understanding or appreciating what you've experienced. Most of us as parents have seen young people act out using inappropriate behavior or language. Beneath the behavior is often the need for attention. A son or daughter may be "screaming out" inside to parents or other adults, "Don't ignore me; I'm a real person; I have feelings too." If the young person doesn't get positive attention, affirming him in some way, he may resort to negative behavior just to get some response, especially if he can really push his parents' buttons and get an emotional, passionate response. That response at least shows that the parents took note. Kids are often comforted just from the fact that their parents care enough to get angry and come back at them. To be ignored ultimately is more painful and more hopeless than being misunderstood or only heard in a stereotypical way.

If hearing is incomplete or inaccurate, at least there is interaction. Acknowledging a person's presence can lead to additional conversation and hopefully more connection. Ignoring a person or group of people is more demeaning. To them it feels like being locked out in the night with the porch light turned off.

The authors of *Divided by Faith* agree:

The collective wounds over race run deep. They need to be healed. And for healing to take place, there will have to be forgiveness. But before there is healing, different racial groups of Americans will also have to stop injuring one another. Vast economic inequalities open deep wounds. Segregation—especially in neighborhoods and schools of unequal quality—opens the wounds further. The fact that Americans' health, life, and death are racialized makes gaping wounds. And the immense divisions between social networks, cultures, and religions not only contribute to the rawness of these wounds, but make their healing that much more difficult.[1]

While these wounds can run both deep and long, most men of color choose not to describe them at any depth to their Anglo acquaintances. They've felt rejected before, and they have little desire to risk further rejection and wounding and pain. They resist any move toward making themselves vulnerable to those whom they believe might wound them again.

"The reality is, there are some details that aren't shared," Ray said. "So the Anglo may not understand the full experience of the man of color as he has been rejected, primarily because of his skin color or ethnicity or language. The person of color is either very or somewhat resistant to sharing his experience; he's leery of getting the same kind of rejection. Now, every person can sense rejection and feel very wounded; but the rejection feels very different when it's based on skin color. The man of color may not want to share his wounding with a person very much like the one who already wounded him." Men of color tend to think, *I've been there, done that—why risk going back on that plank, only to be rejected again?*

Incomplete communication is at least a starting place. It needs to be intentionally pursued, however, lest misunderstandings grow and become interpreted as rejection or judgment of what was shared.

Much of this misunderstanding flows from a failure to grasp the huge differences in social context between this nation's various ethnic and racial groups. Americans like to think that everyone in their country enjoys equal opportunity, but the very structure of society as it has developed over the centuries makes that goal elusive. The perspective that everyone of every race in America has an equal chance to succeed "misses the racialized patterns that transcend and encompass individuals," say the authors of *Divided by Faith*. Furthermore:

> *[Such a perspective] misses that whites can move to most any neighborhood, eat at most any restaurant, walk down most any street, or shop at most any store without having to worry or find out that they are not wanted, whereas African Americans often cannot. This perspective misses that white Americans can be almost certain that when stopped by the police, it has nothing to do with race, whereas African Americans cannot. This perspective misses that whites are assumed to be middle class unless proven otherwise, are not expected to speak for their race, can remain ignorant of other cultures without penalty, and do not have to ask every time something goes wrong if it is due to race.*

. . . This perspective misses that white Americans are far more likely than black Americans to get a solid education, avoid being a victim of crime, and have family and friends with money to help when extra cash is needed for college, a car, or a house. This perspective misses that white Americans are far more likely to have networks and connections that lead to good jobs than are black Americans. This perspective misses that white Americans are more likely to get fair treatment in the court system than are African Americans. And this perspective ultimately misses the truth revealed by Joe Feagin's and Melvin Sikes's exhaustive study of black middle class Americans: "Today blatant, subtle, and covert discrimination against African Americans persists in virtually all aspects of their public life. . . . Racial discrimination is pervasive, and cumulative and costly in its impact." The individualistic perspective encourages people to dismiss such evidence as liberal, wrongheaded, overblown, or as isolated incidents. Such a perspective, then, fails to see or acknowledge, as Cornel West puts it in Race Matters, *"the sheer absurdity that confronts human beings of African descent in this country—the incessant assaults on black intelligence, beauty, character, and possibility."*

Ultimately, such a perspective effectively reproduces racialization. Because its existence is not recognized, action is not taken to overcome it.[2]

And a blind spot strikes again!

Such assaults on ethnic intelligence, beauty, character, and possibility occur all the time. Just a few weeks ago, the classmate of my coworker's seventeen-year-old daughter got sent home from work after she arrived with her hair in cornrows, a popular style among African Americans. Her boss at the fashionable suburban restaurant told her, "You can't work here with that style of hair." Why not? Because it's "too black"?

Most whites have little idea of how powerfully an individual's "blackness" affects his or her opportunities for advancement. Almost universally, the darker the skin, the lower on the social scale the individual lands. This seems to hold true across the world, not only in continental America. Even in Puerto Rico, where skin color runs the gamut, no black person has ever won the governor's chair.

Because suburban and urban Christians don't fully understand one another's experiences, their friendships lack real intimacy—they never reach Level Four—and without the genuine empathy that grows from deep understanding, the relationships usually develop a "disconnect." When the two do not reach a Level Four intimacy that will allow their relationship to mature and grow (see chapter 6), they often see their relationship in completely different terms. The suburban man may think he has built a profound friendship with his urban colleague, while the urban man considers the relationship little more than a surface-level acquaintanceship. In the end, the man of color approaches the relationship with a deep conviction that the two are not coming together on a level playing field.

If true friendship and partnership are ever to develop between men of differing cultural, ethnic, or linguistic groups, they must learn how to build a relationship based on trust and intimate knowledge. That takes time, because they *must* travel through the four levels of relationship: acquaintance, feelings, confidence, and intimacy. And that's not easy to do between people of differing cultures or religious backgrounds.

While such difficulties may seem especially acute between blacks and whites, *any* cross-cultural friendship has to leap over imposing barriers. English-speaking Hispanics sometimes struggle with Spanish-speaking Hispanics. Various Asian communities often have a hard time working cooperatively with one another. Differences in temperaments, in values, in use of language, in customs and expectations and history all can cause a lot of pain. The issue is emphatically *not* just black and white. But it emphatically *does* call for genuine listening. Those in cross-cultural relationships must strive to reach Level Four if they are to effectively identify and address the blind spots that keep us apart.

LISTEN TO UNDERSTAND

The only way to overcome the difficulties and bridge the gap is to learn how to understand the position of someone different from yourself. All of us have to develop the ability to listen to understand.

How often do we truly listen to understand? Usually we listen to *respond*. We open our ears just enough to formulate a reply. But such an approach will not get us very far.

The only way we're going to bridge this gap is to make a connection at the heart—and that occurs only through listening. Some develop this ability by summarizing what they hear others saying. They'll repeat what they thought they heard, then say, "Is that right? Is that what you said?"

Only this kind of listening can transform our churches and our relationships. When we change our grid from "listen to respond," to "listen to understand," we open up possibilities that never before existed.

Such listening encourages honest and open discussion. It makes it easier for an urban pastor to express his pain, and it makes it easier for a suburban pastor to hear it. It encourages a suburban pastor to articulate his desire to minister to the poor, and it encourages an urban pastor to accept that desire as genuine.

Listening to understand requires that we bring everybody to the table. Many times individuals among us develop labels as dissenters or "naysayers." These individuals often share opinions that others consider less than desirable or bring perspectives that others don't want to hear. I think we sometimes mislabel and misunderstand these folk; if anything, they should be called confronters.

We need confronters in the body of Christ. Often they bring empowerment and truth, and many times they fill the biblical role of the prophet. They bring a timely message that, in our natural state, we may fear and oppose. In order for us to move forward, we need to listen—really listen—to the confronter. True listening goes beyond hearing. True listening carries an action component. True listening says, "I'm going to receive what you say, carefully consider it, and act on its truth."

Elliott Greene, one of the few African American members of his five thousand-member congregation, serves the Park Cities Presbyterian Church in Dallas, Texas, as an assistant pastor of discipleship. He knows a lot about the wrong kind of listening. "Too often when we sit down to discuss racial issues, there's a lot more talking than listening," he said. "We need to put ourselves in positions to be able to see these issues from the perspectives of others."[3]

When we listen to understand, we begin to cross the natural barriers to those unlike us. No one can "do justice" without first understanding the real needs of those who need such justice. Justice requires that we understand the needs of others—their current situation, their wounds, their history. And we cannot gain such an understanding without closing our mouths and truly *listening*.

THE IMPORTANCE OF RESPECT

When we begin to truly listen, we may hear stories that will surprise and even shock us. Until we listen, we will never realize how much others need and crave our respect—and how often we have unknowingly failed to give it.

A Filipino pastor came to Denver for a pastors' summit. "We

tried to get an Anglo church to let a Filipino congregation rent its facility," he reported, "but it took a whole year before someone said yes. And when we did get that facility, they didn't want our children running around; they didn't want to smell our food; they didn't want us to do this or that. They gave us what amounted to the Ten Commandments of not violating the sanctity of their worship center."

I have no doubt that the Anglo leaders of that church never realized how their "commands" had so terribly demeaned and disrespected their Filipino brothers. They probably felt they had shown God's love to the Filipino congregation by allowing its members to use their facility—and they had. But more than facilities or resources, all of God's people need *respect* from one another. When respect goes wanting, loving confrontation must take place. I believe that the one injured must find the humility and the fortitude to confront his brother and say, "May I tell you that these rules are offensive to me? Now let me tell you why."

Some who are confronted will hear the truth and repent; others won't. But the one injured has to be willing to confront the issue with integrity. He has to be willing to expose his heart. He has to be willing to say how the comments or actions injured both him and his people. Unfortunately, most of these hurts go unreported—a disservice to both parties.

Before Raleigh Washington came to work with Promise Keepers, he served for several years as the only black pastor in the Evangelical Free Church of America. Several churches in that denomination began contacting him about speaking to their congregations and bringing his choir with him. But once he arrived, he discovered that many pastors began giving him the "Ten Commandments" of what he could and couldn't do at church.

"The Free Church is full of Swedes and Norwegians," one would tell him, "but we have a lot of Germans here. I understand that you like to make a lot of jokes about Swedes and Norwegians—but none of that goes here. And you know, your choir has a tendency to be repetitious at the end of the song. Can you cut them off?"

Several pastors would likewise say, "Raleigh, I've heard you preach before, and man, you're a great preacher. But here, you have to get it all done in twenty-seven minutes." Not twenty-eight minutes or twenty-nine minutes; twenty-seven minutes. That was the law.

For the first year or two, Raleigh complied. But then he began saying, "No more." When some of those pastors called for return visits, he'd say, "You know, you have your Ten Commandments, and I have mine. I can't come unless you allow me to be black. I can't come unless you give me the honor and respect I deserve. You also need to allow my choir the freedom to be black. If you can't tell your congregation, 'Now folks, cut off your beeper, because Raleigh and his folks are going to be here. We're going to give them a little bit more time,' then I won't feel welcome. I'll feel like I'm in a straitjacket."

To their credit, these pastors began listening to understand—and before long they started to hear. Never before had they considered how their "Ten Commandments" had robbed Raleigh and his choir of their God-given respect. But when Raleigh risked confronting his fellow pastors in love and they humbled themselves to hear, a new openness began to develop—an openness that taught both groups, "We have something to give *and* to receive."

How easy it is to dismiss people or their culture simply because you don't understand! Not long ago I visited a church in Charlotte, South Carolina. A group of one hundred or more youth took the stage and started performing a musical set. The music didn't resonate with me, and I was not having a fun time. Just then the pastor leaned over and said to me, "Our kids created all of this music. We don't let them go up front unless they write both the tunes and the words."

His statement completely changed my perspective. Suddenly I noticed how the rest of the body affirmed these kids, how it supported them and tapped into their efforts. I saw the adults connecting with their youth in a way that most churches don't. God revealed a huge personal blind spot to me, allowing me to replace my disdain with respect.

WE NEED EACH OTHER

Too often when the dominant culture provides help or assistance to a community of color, that help comes bundled with pride. "I can do something for you," it says wordlessly, "but I don't expect that you can do anything for me. You need me, but I really don't need you." Very often, it doesn't even realize it is doing this.

The truth is, we all need each other. All of us have something to give, and all of us have something to receive. God has made us interdependent, not independent. Why else would he so often compare the church—the whole church, not merely individual congregations—to a body? So Paul writes, "The eye cannot say to the hand, 'I don't need you!' And the head cannot say to the feet, 'I don't need you!' . . . But God has combined the members of the body and has given greater honor to the parts that lacked it, so that there should be no division in the body, but that its parts should have equal concern for each other" (1 Cor. 12:21, 24-25).

God wants his sons to be doing the work of the kingdom *together*. Interdependence is a major component of justice. We can't do justice alone; we have to have help.

Those in the dominant culture cannot continue to communicate to the communities of color that "you need us, but we don't need you," for that kind of oppression will always keep us apart. Instead, we must learn to say, "I am no better than you;

God made you to be just as good as I am." Either we need each other or God is a liar.

When we come to the table, we recognize our need for one another. We recognize our need to hear one another and listen to one another. The knowledge and education that we gain from each other cannot but enrich us all.

"I like to look at it like this," said Harold Velasquez, vice president of creative services at Promise Keepers. "When my children were babies, I thought it was really about me caring for them. *What could they do for me?* I wondered. But when I look back at it now, I see how my children caused me to grow up. From them I learned unconditional love, patience, and the joy of giving. I discovered that I received much more than anything I gave."

Is this a new message? Hardly. But it's one that we all need to take to heart. We really do need each other, *especially* brothers in Christ from other cultures, ethnicities, and backgrounds. How else can we see and identify the blind spots that keep us separated and the church in trouble?

Music superstar Aretha Franklin has something to say to all of us. "The Queen of Soul" released a song back in 1968 that quickly shot to number seven on the pop charts and number one on the R & B charts. Toward the end of her song "Think," she reminds us:

You need me
And I need you.
Without each other
There ain't nothin' we can do.[4]

Ain't it the truth? Sometimes, the world gets it right before we in the church do. Still, the world lacks the power to fully live it out. The Lord reserves that power for his church.

We really *do* need each other—and every one of us needs the reminder from time to time.

THE EXAMPLE OF JOSEPH

So far as I can see, the *only* way to overcome the blind spots created by differences in cultures and backgrounds is to act on the counsel Joseph gave to his estranged brothers: "Please come near to me" (Gen. 45:4, NKJV).

Joseph's brothers had misunderstood him, mistreated him, oppressed him, and sold him into slavery. For years they told his father he was dead, and so far as they knew, he really was. Yet God remained active in Joseph's life and finally brought him to a place where he could bless the very culture that had abused him.

Joseph brought something to the table that Pharaoh recognized he needed. Without Joseph—and all the life experience that he brought with him, both good and bad—neither Egypt nor the Israelites would have survived. Through Joseph's wisdom, God spared countless lives. And through Joseph's wisdom, God rebuilt a divided family.

I think God wants to do something similar today. And I think he's raised up a "Joseph" to accomplish just that.

On February 13 through 15, 1996, Promise Keepers held a pastors' conference in Atlanta, Georgia. On the third day of the conference, we heard two or three powerful messages on the theme of reconciliation. Afterwards we asked the pastors of color to walk to the front of the Atlanta Dome. As they started forward, the glory of God came down. The Lord visited us in a way I've never seen, before or since. We felt sheer euphoria for forty-five minutes. We felt giddy. We felt ecstatic. We hugged each other relentlessly. Those on the leadership team kept saying to one another, "Can you believe this?" Ask anyone in the arena that day, and he'll tell you: God came.

I believe something deep in the heart of God wanted those

men of color to come forward. Yes, their coming demonstrated the brotherhood of the saints—but I believe it revealed far more than that. God wanted those men up front, before the whole assembled crowd. Why?

Because they're the ones who can lead us to come together.

While the greatest challenge for the suburban church is to recover the justice component of its ministry, the greatest challenge for the urban church is to reach out to its suburban counterparts and to say to them, "Can we partner together in carrying out the kind of justice that delights God's heart?"

America's men of color are the ones, much like Joseph, who have suffered under the heel of the dominant culture. Joseph's brothers may fear to say, "Come near to me"—but Joseph can both say it and mean it. And he *needs* to say it because a famine ravages our land. If he doesn't say it, no one will, and the furious sandstorm we see today will turn into the continental desert of tomorrow.

Come near to me. It sounds good, doesn't it? It appears to be the best way to fulfill one of the Lord's deepest desires: "How good and pleasant it is when brothers live together in unity!" (Ps. 133:1). God wants good and pleasant times to ravish his church, so that both Joseph and his brothers may know God's presence and his favor like never before. Then we will be able say to one another, as Joseph did to his brothers: "'Now therefore, do not be afraid; I will provide for you and your little ones.' And he comforted them and spoke kindly to them" (Gen. 50:21, NKJV).

All that is possible if we, like Joseph and his brothers, will only humble ourselves and "come near."

chapter six
A SHOCKING DISCOVERY

A big surprise awaited me when I left coaching to enter ministry. And it still shocks me today.

In football, coaching staffs always come together for the good of the team. While coaches often disagree at the beginning of the week about how best to attack this defense or stop that offense, by game time, everybody gets on the same page. They never allow disagreements during the week to ruin what they want to do on the weekend.

Beyond that, no coach ever leaves his team midseason for another job, except when everyone deems it in the best interest of the team. If some coach were to announce unexpectedly, "I have another job and I'm gone," you can bet he'd hear the loud chorus, "Hey, you can't leave! We have five more games left!" Such a stunt would reveal an appalling lack of integrity.

It doesn't seem to me as if the same rules govern Christian ministry.

Perhaps I'm missing something—after all, I've spent many more years in coaching than in ministry—but I have noticed what I can only call a shocking spirit of independence in ministry. Before I entered ministry, it never occurred to me that many in the church would leave the team whenever they got "a better offer" or as soon as they suffered an offense, real or imagined. I could be wrong, but that's my honest perception.

"Wait a minute," we say to the one leaving. "Don't you need to come to us first? Don't you need to say, 'Do we agree that it's my time to leave?'"

"No," comes the defiant answer. "I've got to go; God called me. I heard his call, it's real clear to me, and my wife and I agree—so I'm gone." I felt dumbfounded the first time I encountered such a scenario.

Ministry, unlike coaching, appears to have no accepted protocol for making personnel changes. People just say, "God spoke." And who's to say he didn't?

My football career never led me to expect what I commonly find in ministry. And I wonder, *How can that be?* When guys put themselves first and the team second, where's the integrity? Shouldn't ministry set the standard for integrity?

INTEGRITY AS WHOLENESS

What is integrity? The most basic definition derives from the root word, *integer:* "a whole number, as distinguished from a fraction; a complete entity." Integrity is therefore wholeness, completeness, a "soundness of moral character."[1]

Integrity in the church requires that we be honest with and considerate to the whole body. We cannot have integrity without considering and acting in the best interests of the whole church. Integrity does not allow me to make decisions solely on the basis of what will most benefit me or my family or my little group. Integrity demands that we think and act in such a way as to bring wholeness and completeness to the entire body.

When we develop the kind of integrity that God wants for all of his children, we learn to willingly accept direction, protection, and correction. When integrity becomes a part of our lives, we eagerly submit to the truth that we hear. When we make integrity a priority, we pray for revelation in those areas in which others say we are blind. "Let a righteous man strike me—it is a kindness," says the psalmist. "Let him rebuke me—it is oil on my head. My head will not refuse it" (Ps. 141:5).

Where true integrity exists, an exchange such as the following will never take place: "I can't join you," someone says, "because I refuse to compromise truth."

"Okay," we reply, "you're right. God has spoken to you about this issue. So set the parameters for us. Draw up the nonnegotiables. Set the standard and let's agree to it. Then let's rally around these things and come together."

So the speaker goes away, sets the parameters, and returns. We look over the guidelines and say, "We agree to these, just as you wrote them up. Now let's come together."

A silent pause.

"Well," he says, "I don't know if we can come together. But it's good that you agree." (See Matt. 11:16-19.)

Do you see the lack of integrity? I hope you do. I see it, and it makes me want to explode!

Integrity means wholeness, completeness. It means that we jettison independence for interdependence. It requires that we put aside our petty differences in order to serve the Lord together as members of one holy family (see 1 Pet. 2:9).

A concern for integrity compelled the apostle Paul to write, "I plead with Euodia and I plead with Syntyche to agree with each other in the Lord" (Phil. 4:2). These women had contended at the apostle's side "in the cause of the gospel" (v. 3) yet somehow had suffered a personal split. Paul refused to ignore the situation; he could not allow it to go unchallenged. Integrity demanded that he try to bring wholeness and completeness even to a personal division between friends.

Can it require any less of us? Can it require any less of God's chosen shepherds? I believe that an independent spirit generates blind spots that cause God's heart to grieve for integrity in ministry.

NO INTEGRITY WITHOUT ALL OF US

We're all in the body. Paul put it like this: "Here there is no Greek or Jew, circumcised or uncircumcised, barbarian, Scythian, slave or free, but Christ is all, and is in all" (Col. 3:11).

Because the apostle so deeply believed in the message of Christian unity, he confronted Peter, "the Rock," when the latter lost sight of it. "When Peter came to Antioch, I opposed him to his face," writes Paul, "because he was clearly in the wrong. Before certain men came from James, he used to eat with the Gentiles. But when they arrived, he began to draw back and separate himself from the Gentiles" (Gal. 2:11-12). Paul chose integrity over comfort and so confronted Peter over his ungodly split from the minority Gentile believers.

We shouldn't be too hard on old Peter because the truth is, what he did, most of us do at one time or another. Much of the time we unwittingly turn our backs on our friends from other cultures because of style issues. If we're used to a quiet and serene worship service, we may get irritated by a loud and enthusiastic service in which singers repeat the same choruses for long stretches of time. If we don't understand both our tendencies and the culture of our friends, we may allow style differences to begin to separate us.

God calls us to work and minister together. And that's why it hurts so much when our integrity slips and we leave out some members of Christ's body.

A short while ago Promise Keepers flew several members of the Asian community to our headquarters to discuss this very issue. "We have no voice in the machinery of the church in America," they told us. "No one wants our opinion. No one asks for our opinion, and we have no influence outside our own people group."

What's wrong with this picture? It lacks integrity. Wholeness and completeness have vanished from it.

We held similar meetings with members of the Native American community. "You will not find a Native American in a position of authority in any denomination or parachurch group—including Promise Keepers," they said. That hurt, but they were right. They suffer from deep wounds. Since that meeting we have addressed their grievance.

Messianic Jewish groups tell us, "We're just a body of believers who are suffering greatly as we stand for the cause of Christ. And we stand alone." My heart aches when I ponder this. How easily pastors from urban and suburban, black and white, Native American, Hispanic, Asian, (you name it) churches could reach out to Messianic Jewish leaders, could include Messianic Jewish congregations in all kinds of activities. Who can tell what blessings we're missing by forgetting our Messianic Jewish brethren?

How can we expect the church to grow and prosper when we suffer from such a dreadful lack of integrity? Every week, it seems, we see another example of what we're doing to each other. It has to stop.

If the church is to move forward, it needs to do so in integrity. And that requires wholeness, completeness, and that we be of one mind regarding our mutual standing in the family of God.

A FIRST STEP

I have been as guilty as anyone in failing to minister with full integrity. Therefore we have begun a new practice at Promise Keepers that is designed to help us maintain our integrity.

Today we try not to start a single executive meeting without reminding ourselves of Mark 11:25. In that verse Jesus says, "And when you stand praying, if you hold anything against anyone, forgive him, so that your Father in heaven may forgive you your sins." We also remind ourselves of Psalm 66:18, which says, "If I regard iniquity in my heart, the Lord will not hear" (NKJV). And we apply a verse particularly addressed to husbands and wives to our own Level Three and Four relationships: "Husbands, likewise, dwell with them with understanding, giving honor to the wife, as to the weaker vessel, and as being heirs together of the grace of life, that your prayers may not be hindered" (1 Pet. 3:7, NKJV).

Then the meeting leader says something like, "If you have anything against anybody, we can't go on. Please leave the room, because we have no integrity with you here. Now, if you agree that you have clean hands and a pure heart, then let's proceed. Each of us in this room agrees to honor each individual who speaks. We will listen to him, value what he's saying, consider his input, and honor his contribution."

As an open and honest exchange takes place, the Spirit of God moves in power. Without such a commitment to integrity, those of us from the dominant culture often have a difficult time listening to what may be hard for us to hear or somehow unclear.

It works the other way, too. If three men of color on an executive board meet off-site, develop an agenda, and try to enforce it at the board meeting without disclosure—then they lack integrity and they dishonor the Lord. But if they meet elsewhere, have a private discussion, and come into the meeting saying, "We've met and we feel this way," that does show integrity. Integrity includes, honors, and respects others.

When we conduct meetings with integrity, when everyone agrees to the same biblical standards, I believe God can trust us with his business. For the church to thrive, there has to be a genuine respect and a mutual harmony between all of God's children. And that requires incorruptible character.

True Christian unity, of course, doesn't come by ignoring differences or by considering theological disagreements to be relatively unimportant. In fact, healthy disagreement is vital to the well-being of the church. It creates an environment that fosters new ways of seeing things and helps us to uncover deadly blind spots. When I say, "No dissension, no discussion," I mean that without disagreement, we won't discuss the very issues that must be explored if we are to move ahead. It's not only *okay* when people disagree; it's crucial.

When we (at Promise Keepers) begin to insist that everybody at the table agree with us, serious blind spots come into play. Many of us harbor extensive assumptions and a propensity to think that our ideas about leadership, ministry, lifestyle, and the use of resources are either biblically begotten or intuitively obvious. If we really open up, we're going to see these assumptions cut apart by others who also hold their ideas to be self-evident. "Faithful are the wounds of a friend; but the kisses of an enemy are deceitful" (Prov. 27:6).

"Iron sharpeneth iron; so a man sharpeneth the countenance of his friend" (Prov. 27:17, KJV). God wants us to welcome differing opinions; but the openness, faith, courage, and patience required to achieve a conciliatory decision do not come easily. Developing them is harder than pulling teeth, probably more akin to pulling your own teeth! Every time we sit down together, we should strive to hear all sides of the debate. If wisdom comes from a multitude of counselors (see Prov. 15:22), then no one can gain wisdom by dominating the discussion. Albert Einstein once said, "No problem is solved from the same consciousness that created it."

Out of our disagreements—if we keep our poise and integrity—we will find the solutions. But if we silence those who disagree with us, if they fear to speak up, we will never tap into the fresh ideas that God in his grace has put into the room.

WHEN YOU FAIL

Even when we become sensitized to the issues of integrity, we can still come up short. We've certainly found this to be true at Promise Keepers.

Recently an angry representative from a group of Asian pastors called us to complain about our own insensitivity. We had scheduled a PK event at almost the same time and in the same city where this group planned to hold its very first pastors' conference. The men worried that our event would overwhelm theirs. It especially incensed them that no one from our ministry had called to ask for their input.

Guilty as charged. We had a lapse in integrity.

So what does one do in such a case? One immediately asks for forgiveness. We agreed, "Let's quickly tell them that they are right. We're wrong. We dishonored them by not getting their counsel on the date of our event, as well as other details. It's true that we are locked in now, but we want to make sure that they understand what's going to happen from here on out. Let's tell them, 'We've been told that you have no voice; you have a voice now. We propose that you come from your meeting united in what you would like to say to the dominant culture. Tell them how many times you've been left out, like we just left you out.'"

When you fail, the only thing you can do is to get authentic, ask for forgiveness, and try not to make the same mistakes again. If you need to make some changes in the way you do business, make them. That's what we're trying to do right now.

IF IT'S BROKEN, FIX IT

Originally the board of Promise Keepers had very little representation from America's ethnic communities. Once we recognized that deficiency, we took steps to incorporate a member from each major racial grouping on our board of directors. Today our board has more people of color than it does Anglos. Why is this important? Now my ethnic brother, a kind of stranger in Egypt (see Gen. 15:13), can point out things that I would never see.

Today, whenever the board votes, the men of color have every opportunity to carry the vote. Our executive cabinet also has a majority of people of color among its voting members. So in every vote taken at Promise Keepers, from the board through the executive cabinet, people of color can carry the vote if they so choose. It's a way to guarantee that their voice will not be quashed.

"For many years," says Harold Velasquez, vice president of creative services at Promise Keepers, "when Promise Keepers would talk about reconciliation, it looked to us as if it was just a black and white issue and that we weren't given a voice at the table. From what I've seen in the last couple of years, the ministry has been very intentional about trying to make sure that all the other camps have representation. Certainly inroads have been made, and we're making progress. Are we there yet? No. Are we getting there? Our hope is, yes."

As an organization, the current workforce at Promise Keepers is about 38 percent diverse. We still have a ways to go—we're not kidding ourselves; we know this problem is deep—but any progress we have made has come out of intentional decision making.

How far do we have yet to go? Perhaps we got a clue a few months ago. After we held a black-awareness chapel, our point man received a blistering e-mail from an irate staff person opposed to the program. Now understand, racial reconciliation has been a heartbeat for Promise Keepers since the ministry began. It shocked many of us that such a thing could still happen within our organization. But I think it emphasized for all of us that this is an issue in progress. To have integrity in our work and message, we constantly have to work within our own walls, because issues remain even there. At the same time, though, I know we've come a long way. Five years ago, we received twenty e-mails!

GET BACK UP AND INTO THE GAME

In football, when someone knocks you down, you pick yourself up off the field and get back into the game. If you get knocked down twice, you get up twice. If you get knocked down fifteen times, you get up fifteen times. Legendary coach Vince Lombardi is credited with saying, "It's not whether you get knocked down, it's whether you get up."

When I moved from coaching to ministry, it surprised me how widely this attitude was missing. Too often when someone gets knocked down in ministry these days, you've lost them. In the past few years, Promise Keepers has reduced its staff significantly, so there are a lot of wounded people out there . . . the people who came to Colorado in faith and then found themselves unemployed, for instance. I know that many of them have distanced themselves from me, something for which I must take responsibility. When I see them, they can hardly stand to look at me. Don't misunderstand me; I don't blame them because I know I did some things wrong. At times I crossed the line. And when you cross the line with some believers—when you're involved in a play that knocks them down—they're "out of here." In sports, we get back up, slap five, and go back to the game. I see a seasoned temperament in sports that too often seems missing in the church.

Is this, too, an issue of integrity? I believe it is. If integrity means wholeness and completeness—if the success of the team means more than the accomplishments of the individual—then "getting back in the game" truly is an issue of integrity.

COURAGE AND TENACITY

It takes boldness, courage, and tenacity to live a life of integrity. And it takes an extra dose of all three when you're trying hard to overcome the current divisions in the church.

"Let's face it," said Ed Barron, vice president of U.S. ministries at Promise Keepers, "people have been hacking at this thing for a long time; it's cost some their life. And I'm sure it will cost others their life before it's all said and done."

For the most part, of course, God doesn't call on us to give up our lives in order to maintain our Christian integrity. Yet he may call on us to lovingly confront our brothers who wander from God's commitment to integrity.

"I think it takes boldness, courage, and tenacity on the part of the urban pastor—who comes to the table with pain, with hurts, with feelings of abuse—to be willing to make statements that address blind spots," said one African American minister I'll call Victor. "You have to realize that you may be risking any relationship you might have with your suburban brother."

As an urban pastor himself, Victor knew that if he risked such a confrontation, he might be risking financial support for his ministry. Victor tells of a suburban pastor who became enamored with the ministry of Victor's inner-city church. This pastor frequently brought service groups halfway across the country. Victor describes him as "very, very supportive of the ministry."

But then something happened that almost ruined their relationship.

"This pastor couldn't get over the giftedness of my music minister and sought to recruit him behind my back," Victor recalls. "He even offered him a position. After our church found out, we had a meeting with him where we used the metaphor of feeling raped. Then we spent another hour and a half explaining what this meant and how difficult it was to get someone to minister in an inner-city, ethnic church. He was offering almost twice as much as we could pay. I told him that what he did was to disrespect me; he should have talked to me because we had a close relationship. It blew him out of the water, so much so that he said, through tears, 'I never felt whipped like this, in all the days of my life. I have to go pray.'"

Victor felt sure that he could kiss that relationship—and the support that accompanied it—good-bye. Even so, he felt he had no choice but to confront what he took to be a blatant lack of integrity.

When this man returned, he did so repentantly, "in sackcloth and ashes," as Victor puts it. He thanked Victor for revealing his blind spot and begged the forgiveness of the church. Not only did the relationship not blow up, it continued and matured.

You *have* to deal with hard issues like these, or there's no integrity. If you slither away instead of confronting the issues, you lack integrity.

As we begin to understand each other, appreciate one another, and refuse to allow for a lack of integrity between each other, we gain greater understanding and knowledge. As a result, our love for one another increases.

Make no mistake: these issues are volatile, and the only way we will ever get to such conversations is through a commitment to love. Tough issues surface all the time in cross-cultural and cross-racial relationships. You can't get past them—at least, not while keeping your integrity intact.

WHAT COULD WE DO AS ONE?

I'm fascinated by a single verse of Scripture from the Old Testament. The verse describes not a good thing, but a bad thing—and yet suggests a way to something terrifically good that blesses God's own heart.

"Behold," said the Lord, describing the people living in the time before the Tower of Babel, "they are one people . . . and now nothing which they purpose to do will be impossible for them" (Gen. 11:6, NASB).

Because these people purposed to do only evil, however, the Lord reached down from heaven and confused their language, "that they may not understand one another's speech" (v. 7). Mankind has accomplished many great feats since that day, yet never again did God say of the race, "Now nothing that they propose to do will be impossible for them." Why not? Because never again did he say of them, "Indeed the people are one" (v. 6, NKJV).

What power there is in unity! What creativity, what know-how, what strength! While the Lord never again made the people of the world one, he *has* made the people of the church one: "Make every effort to keep the unity of the Spirit through the bond of peace. There is one body and one Spirit—just as you were called to one hope when you were called—one Lord, one faith, one baptism; one God and Father of all, who is over all and through all and in all" (Eph. 4:3-6).

What mighty things could the church accomplish if its members made a wholehearted commitment to integrity—to wholeness and completeness—and began to live out the "one faith" that we profess? Would anything that we propose to do be withheld from us?

If it is true, as Jesus said, that, "If two of you on earth agree about anything you ask for, it will be done for you by my Father in heaven" (Matt. 18:19), then what might happen if *the whole church* came together, praying with integrity for the Lord to shake our nation and our world with the limitless power of his Spirit?

I don't know. But I'd like to find out.

chapter seven FOUR OF
A KIND BEATS A FULL HOUSE

At virtually every Promise Keepers event I attend, I sit in the front row. I sit there for no other reason than to make myself accessible to men.

Frequently a guy will come up to me, extend his hand, and say something like, "Coach, I want you to know that this movement has changed my life. Three years ago I was headed down the wrong road. And I just want to thank you for being faithful."

Routinely I'll answer, "Thank you. Now, can I ask you a big favor?"

"Yeah," the man says, "ask me anything, Coach."

"Pray for me, would you?" I reply. "Pray for my family. Pray for us at Promise Keepers."

I realize that if we're going to keep our fresh fire and energy and vision, we

must have the protection of prayer. A spiritual battle rages between the forces of heaven and hell, and we can't afford to enter the fight without committed prayer warriors encircling us.

A NECESSITY FOR LEADERS

Everyone who wants to make a lasting difference for Christ and his kingdom has to find a way to build and maintain an effective prayer covering. Failure in ministry can often be traced to failure to create an active, unified prayer team. When we disregard or neglect the crucial place of group prayer, we allow our blind spots to continue to plague and injure us.

With a committed prayer team laboring for and with us, however, we tap into the infinite power of God. We begin to see his mind and his will with increasing clarity. We feel his heartbeat with growing certainty. More and more, his desires become our desires, and we see his mighty hand acting on our behalf and for his glory.

Jesus promises us, "If you abide in Me, and My words abide in you, you will ask what you desire, and it shall be done for you. By this My Father is glorified, that you bear much fruit; so you will be My disciples" (John 15:7-8, NKJV). Our Lord tells us that when we abide in him—when we vitally connect to him in righteousness—then he answers our prayers and we "bear much fruit"—we carry out the justice that delights his heart. And in that way, God is glorified.

Probably no apostle enjoyed a more productive ministry career than Paul; and judging from the letters of the New Testament, no apostle asked others to pray for him more than Paul. A coincidence? I doubt it.

"And pray for us, too, that God may open a door for our message, so that we may proclaim the mystery of Christ," he wrote to the Colossians (4:3). "Brothers, pray for us," he directed the Thessalonians (1 Thess. 5:25). "Finally, brothers, pray for us that the message of the Lord may spread rapidly and be honored, just as it was with you. And pray that we may be delivered from wicked and evil men, for not everyone has faith," he asked them again (2 Thess. 3:1-2).

(And if he wrote the book of Hebrews, as many suspect, he also made the identical request of them. See Hebrews 13:18.)

But what kind of prayer should we request?

BACK TO MARK 11:25

The same verse that guides our meetings at Promise Keepers also directs our times of prayer. Remember Mark 11:25? Jesus said, "And when you stand praying, if you hold anything against anyone, forgive him, so that your Father in heaven may forgive you your sins."

Without clean hands and a pure heart, our prayers go no higher than the ceiling. But when we come together to pray according to a set of mutually agreeable ground rules, and when we refuse to begin without first making sure that we follow our Lord's command, watch out! The sky's the limit.

In the game of poker, four of a kind beats a full house every time.[1] The same principle holds true for prayer. More power exists in the prayers of four believers who petition God in unity than in a house full of believers who pray with clashing agendas and attitudes.

This principle helps us to set some useful ground rules. Before we pray in groups, we say, "Remember, our prayers are going to be voided if anyone here has anything against anybody in this room, or against anybody else." One of the first times we began this way, at least two members of our team left the room to get squared away with other staff members.

Because God loves to honor his Word, we continue to see the fruit of praying in groups according to Mark 11:25. As we emphasize restored and godly relationships as a precondition for effective prayer, we pray with far more genuineness and power. And we see more results.

Do you want to know one reason why the *growing divide* continues to afflict the American church? I would like to suggest it's because there has been no integrity when we pray. One part of the church has "held something against" the other part, and neither part has learned how to forgive the other. How can the Lord hear and answer our prayers for revival when the church remains seriously divided? When we ask him for revival, which part do we want him to revive?

The prayer component of any Christian organization or group has to rise at least to the level of purity described in the books of Leviticus or Numbers or Deuteronomy. Moses told his people that if they wanted God to hear their prayers, they had to obey the Lord and surrender to his will. The same remains true for us.

THE CHURCH'S BOILER ROOM

Group prayer, offered with integrity, is the boiler room of the church. There we tap into God's power. Without integrity in our praying, our prayer rooms are reduced to mere noise.

It takes only one person whose heart is not right, who knowingly fails to resolve a conflict with another, to nullify the power of group prayer. Let's say we fill a prayer room with representatives from several distinct camps, whether theological, ethnic, or cultural. A few minutes into the meeting, someone starts praying in tongues. A conservative believer hears the ecstatic utterance and feels grieved. What happens? The whole room shuts down.

When we feel offended by the way someone prays—let's change the image and say that an individual starts dancing, or raising his hands, or speaking in Russian—our negative reaction turns off the spiritual power in the room. We shut down the entire proceedings.

Or consider a more concrete example. A current dispute in the Native American community concerns the use of drums in worship. Many conservatives consider any role for drums inappropriate since in times past the drums were given names and thought to be possessed by spirits. Many other believers, however, feel that the drums represent a distinctive characteristic of their culture and insist that as long as the drums aren't given names or possessed by spirits, their use in Christian worship services ought to be allowed. What happens if this issue isn't resolved ahead of time and one or the other group feels offended by what happens in the prayer meeting? The whole room shuts down.

To prevent such a thing from happening, we have begun to implement some ground rules for group prayer. Dave Wardell and Rose Opp lead our prayer ministry, and I credit them with increasing the effectiveness of our Promise Keepers event prayer rooms.

How does it work? Suppose you see a group of individuals praying in a room. You don't enter the room right away. You stop at station number one, which challenges you to check your heart and consider whether you have any unresolved issues with someone else. If you're clear, you move to station number two, which explains the guidelines that direct how believers should pray in that room. "If you don't agree to these guidelines," it says, "don't come in." Once you clear stations one and two, you're welcome to enter the room and join the others already in prayer.

A short while ago Promise Keepers invited about sixty intercessors from around the country, representing a wide variety of camps, to join us at our headquarters for three days of sustained prayer. We brought them in for the expressed purpose of discussing what it takes to create and maintain an effective prayer room. We told them, "Whenever we pray together, here are the ground rules. If you can't agree to these ground rules, then we must ask you to leave." They agreed, and we enjoyed three stunning days of prayer.[2]

Out of those meetings, we identified several key aspects to effective group prayer. First, everyone must come in humility; a proud heart cannot pray effectively. Second, every man in the room—regardless of ethnic, theological, or cultural background—must prefer others over himself. Third, everyone must remain consciously sensitive to the differing styles and theological convictions present in the room. Fourth, no one may "push" their own style. And fifth, everyone must learn to function within a mold comfortable to all present. In short, everyone must be of one accord and come to the Lord of glory on an absolutely equal footing.

Do we want to pray effectively in groups? Then let's check our hearts. What prevents or inhibits us from flowing freely in God's presence? If we are to have any chance of bringing the church back together, it's going to take extraordinary prayer. And remember: the tremendous power that issues from effective group prayer comes from the unity of those who pray.

I LOVE MY JOB

On February 7, 2002, we hosted a group of about six hundred men (pastors made up about 40 percent of the crowd) in Washington, D.C. We wanted to encourage pastors all across the country to form a prayer team of men led by a pastor-appointed, male prayer leader. We hope to raise up at least thirty thousand of these special leaders.

Pastor Ted Haggard of New Life Church in Colorado Springs rose to speak. "There isn't anything about being a pastor that doesn't thrill my heart," he said. "I love all of it. I've been called by God, and I get to do just what he's gifted me to do. I love preaching. I love counseling. I love funerals. I love weddings. I love fights. I love every aspect of my job. I love it all."

As I looked into the crowd, I could see startled, disbelieving looks on hundreds of faces. You could almost hear them thinking: *I wish I could say that!*

At one point the speaker pointed to a man sitting in the crowd.

"Do you see that guy right over there?" he asked. "That's my pastor-appointed prayer leader. Do you know what he's done? This guy is on fire for the Lord. He's gone around and rallied the men of our church to pray for me 24/7. I'm covered. My family's covered. The enemy can't get to me. That's why I'm able to enjoy what I do so much."

A little later in the program, this pastor's prayer leader came forward to speak. From the moment he opened his mouth, you could tell he had two distinct qualities: fresh fire and deep humility. This guy was *alive*. He breathed excitement over prayer. And he painted a thrilling picture of what it's like to recruit a guy and motivate him to pray. He described how a guy grows and stretches through prayer. He emphasized that his job was to serve his pastor through prayer. His task was not to counsel, to correct, to advise, or to tell his pastor how to do his job. His sole assignment was to get men in his church to pray.

Sounds good, doesn't it? So why not bless yourself with such a team?

I believe that every pastor needs a male, pastor-appointed prayer leader. That man has only one job: to recruit other men from the church to join a prayer team for the sole purpose of praying for the pastor, for the needs of the church, and for the community. That's the total assignment.

CREATING YOUR OWN MALE PRAYER TEAM

Every man, every boy, grows up longing to be part of a team. In his heart, every man yearns to be picked as a member of a winning squad.

For his part, every pastor and church leader needs loyal teammates who will surround and assist him. Most of the pastors I know feel isolated. Often their isolation leads to deep wounds and awful loneliness.

Enter the team!

Pastors and church leaders need teams of men around them. And men want to be part of a team. What better way to meet both needs than to create teams of godly men who pray faithfully for their pastor or leader, church, and community?

Do you know the story of the redwood tree? A redwood tree, when it grows to maturity, reaches a height of a hundred feet. But the roots of a redwood tree rarely go deeper than six inches to a foot into the ground. So why doesn't a mild wind topple a redwood? It's because the roots of individual redwood trees embrace and intertwine. They grab on to one another and never let go. That's how redwoods stand—they stand *together*. Like a team.

Pastor, do you realize the critical importance of a male prayer leader who recruits other men to surround you and cover you with prayer? A team of faithful prayer warriors cannot help but enhance your ability to lead.

We do not at all intend to undermine or demean the ministry of faithful women who for years have labored as effective prayer warriors. Rather, as a ministry focused on men, we seek to show men their God-ordained role in supporting their pastor and other leaders in prayer.

WE'RE GOING TO DO IT TOGETHER

Former Michigan football coach Bo Schembechler often said to his teams, "Do you know how we're going to win? We're going to master the fundamentals. We're going to block and tackle better than everyone. We're going to throw and catch better than anyone. We're going to protect the football. And we're going to do it *together*. That's how we're going to do it. There are going to be no superstars on this team. Everybody is going to be more interested in Michigan than in himself. That's how we're going to win."

Let me ask you a few questions. Have you ever requested that one of your men undertake to pray specifically, regularly, and passionately for you? Have you ever asked anyone to start a prayer team like the one I described? What do you imagine would happen if a male, pastor-appointed prayer leader called some of your men and asked, "Can I take you to lunch?" then sat down with each one, talked with each of them about the Lord, developed a kindred spirit, and explained, "Here's what we need you to do in this church"? I have no doubt that many, if not most, men would jump at the chance. There would be many who would say, "How high? How far? How much? Tell me what you want me to do. I'm ready."

But nobody asks these guys.

I say there are men all over the church who could transform our congregations if someone would just mobilize them. If we are ever to get the church together, if we are ever to heal the growing divide that plagues the church—then pastors *must* learn how to get their men into the game. Women, for the most part, are already lined up on the field. It's the men we have to enlist, engage, and get active.

Just yesterday, the head coach of a major college basketball team called me at home. He's a believer under tremendous pressure.

"Man," he told me, "I'm praying. I've been offered another job and I don't know whether to take it." Then he described his whole difficult situation.

"Here's what you need," I told him. "We are going to build a team of men around you who understand Mark 11:25 and who are going to cover you. And you're going to discover that in the midst of pressure and circumstances and everything else, you can find breathing room."

We need to create such prayer teams for our brothers, especially for guys in high-profile positions in which the media scrutinizes and reports everything they do. I hear the words of the prophet Samuel ringing in my ears. "As for me," he told his people, "far be it from me that I should sin against the Lord by failing to pray for you" (1 Sam. 12:23). I envision putting teams of prayer around these leaders—teams of men who will love them and encourage them, not tell them how to do their jobs. These prayer warriors will say, "We are your brothers in Christ. We're proud of you, and we want you to be free to be the leader that God has raised you up to be." I envision this happening everywhere. And as soon as we take on the burden of another, we begin to feel his pain and struggle, and the experience knits us together. Periodically, we'll feel compelled to call this brother to encourage him.

When pastors and church leaders form these prayer teams, they'll discover the freedom and power of concentrated prayer. Not only that, they'll discover a new ability to draw out of their men a higher level of spirituality and productivity that infuses them with a sense of worth and value, mission, and vision.

And you know the best thing of all? Every leader can have such a prayer team. He just has to take the initiative to make it happen.

NABBING EAGLES

When I first came to the University of Colorado in 1982, I faced a difficult challenge. The football program had fallen on hard times—it had won only seven games in three years—and we had to begin the hard work of rebuilding the program.

Yet by 1990, just eight years later, the Associated Press had voted us the national champions. How did we do it? By attracting eagles.

An eagle is an athlete who stands out. He's not only an

achiever, he's an overachiever. In the world of evangelism, Billy Graham and Luis Palau are eagles. In the world of acting, Morgan Freeman and Tom Cruise are eagles.

For the most part, eagles like to flock together. If you can get one eagle, you can get another eagle. The problem was, before 1982, the University of Colorado Buffaloes hadn't attracted any eagles for a long time. So what could we do? We prayed and consecrated the football program to Jesus Christ.

Before long God gave us Eric McCarty, a true eagle and a genuine fireball. From that day on, whenever we brought in key recruits, we put them with Eric. He loved people, he loved God, and he had great chemistry with young kids. Eric became a catalyst for us to attract other eagles. And soon we started getting the kind of talent that all great teams must attract and keep.

Eagles attract eagles. That principle works not only in football, but in most other spheres of life. It certainly works in ministry and in the area of prayer.

If you want to experience the difference that a team of male prayer warriors can make in your ministry, then find yourself an eagle. Find a humble man in your church who loves God and others, who knows how to pray, who's filled with the Spirit—and challenge him to recruit other men to serve on a team dedicated to prayer.

Did you know that in any average group of one hundred men, eighty can be influenced by the actions of ten others? Ten men in any such a group will naturally influence the others in a positive direction, while the remaining ten will resist and oppose virtually every positive thing presented. Your task is to find those ten positive eagles and invest in them, train them, and set them loose to influence the others.

Believe me, nothing is more fun than being with men of God who love God and who get together to do the things that men of God like to do. That is pure fellowship.

So get yourself an eagle. Let him attract other eagles. Get them praying for you, for your church, and for your community. And then stand back and watch as God begins to remove the blind spots that keep us from approaching his throne as a unified family of believers.

When that happens, you're off and soaring into the wild blue yonder.

chapter eight TAKE ME
WHERE I CAN'T TAKE MYSELF

When a blue-chip high school athlete looks around at different colleges, what factors help him to choose a school? Most kids consider several variables: location, school size, winning tradition, community culture, etc. But one of the biggest factors comes down to coaching. Most athletes look for a program where they can learn.

It's as if they say, "Coach me. Please, coach me. Take me beyond myself. Take me where I can't take myself." A good coach develops the ability to take his athletes where they can't take themselves.

This is a definition not only of good coaching, but also of good pastoring. Successful pastors take guys where they can't go by themselves. Effective pastors understand why a guy isn't responding and go after him. They see Jesus Christ in

him, the hope of glory. And they know that man is a dynamo just waiting to be unleashed for the kingdom.

But what's the best way to tap into such vast potential? I've noticed that pastors who try to minister from a distance never "get" most of their guys. Successful pastors go down to where their guys are, understand where they come from, and take them to where they always wanted to go (even if they never knew how to get there).

No man, however, will go anywhere with anyone unless he first develops a committed, long-term relationship with an individual who can take him where he can't go by himself. The foundation to success in any team activity is relationship.

FOUR QUADRANTS

A study done several years ago by the University of Minnesota investigated the most common types of leaders in America. Dr. Dennis B. Guernsey used the grid on the next page to help investigators evaluate different leadership styles. Every leader falls somewhere within the grid.

LEADERSHIP BASED ON RELATIONSHIP

Leaders with high control set and maintain clear boundaries; leaders with low control have few or unclear boundaries. Leaders with high love constantly communicate their concern and compassion to their followers.

A resolute leader sets and maintains clear boundaries, and he blends his pursuit of superior results with kindness. He monitors his followers carefully. He pays attention to all aspects of his relationships. Other kinds of leaders do not have many boundaries, and those they do have are confusing. Such leaders tend to treat their underlings more like projects than people.

Some leaders condone mistakes and avoid confrontation. Have you heard the saying, "Love without truth is hypocrisy"?

HIGH CONTROL
(CLEAR BOUNDARIES)

AUTHORITATIVE
- Pursuit of excellence
- Compassionate
- Decisive

AUTHORITARIAN
- Overbearing
- Stern and rigid
- Unreasonable
- Domineering

HIGH LOVE

LOW LOVE

PERMISSIVE
- Lenient
- Intentionally overlooks error
- Indecisive
- Reluctant to confront

NEGLECTFUL
- Careless
- Disregard
- Unmindful

LOW CONTROL
(UNCLEAR BOUNDARIES)

While a leader like this is hamstrung by hypocrisy, he still proba-bly outperforms leaders who fail to take care of business. Low control inevitably gives rise to unclear boundaries. He has no idea who's on first; he probably stops at the bar (or at the committee meeting, or at the drama rehearsal, or at a deacon's house) on the way home. But as bad as he can be, he's not the worst leader (or the worst parent or pastor or coach). That dubious distinction belongs to the authoritarian leader.

This dictatorial leadership style is easily recognized: "My way or the highway." He incarnates the saying, "Truth without love is brutality." He may be right when he corrects others, but he does it without compassion or sensitivity. He's a brute. (Of course, some individuals see even resolute leaders as authoritarian because they recoil from confrontation of any kind.)

My point? A successful coach has to know what kind of home his players come out of. He has to know what life has served up to each kid. If a young man grew up in a lenient and indulgent home, the coach has to assume that no one has ever confronted the young man. If he stayed out beyond curfew at home, his dad just turned his back. The coach has to help that young athlete understand that he needs boundaries—and that the coaching staff will provide them. But he also lets the kid know that these boundaries are going to take him from good to great.

At the University of Colorado, African Americans made up more than half of my team—and Boulder is lily white. Nothing in Boulder suggests to an urban kid that he belongs there, that he's in the right place at the right time. When he enters a restaurant in town, he doesn't see a picture of anything from his culture that validates him as a person of color.

So what did we do? We hired five black coaches and four white coaches. We recruited adults who understood these guys and where they came from. When our athletes grew frustrated, disappointed, or exasperated, our coaches could help get them grounded once more.

The same principles apply to any relationship. To relate effectively to anyone, you have to understand the individual with whom you desire a relationship. The only way to successfully relate to anyone is to understand whom God has put into your care. Understanding is the first key to any successful relationship.

R-E-L-A-T-E

A simple acrostic helps me to develop and improve my own relationships: R-E-L-A-T-E.

R stands for *respect*. Every man deserves respect. Peter writes, "Show proper respect to everyone" (1 Pet. 2:17). God created all of us to be significant; you've never met anyone who didn't want to feel significant. We don't give respect because of performance or accomplishment or behavior, but because every human being is created in the image of God. We *afford* respect; no one has to *earn* it. Yet the culture (and sometimes the church) often teaches that we must earn respect. Wherever the dominant culture disregards the truth that respect is afforded, not earned, believers must more consciously put it into practice. Disrespect can lead not only to hurt feelings and anger but also to suicide.

E is for *encouragement.* John Maxwell reports that by the time Theodore Roosevelt had reached twelve years of age, his father saw that his son hadn't developed physically. Teddy had very poor eyesight and looked weak and frail. His dad said, "Son, you have the mind, but you don't have the body. You have to develop your body, otherwise your mind won't go as far as it could and should." As a result, Roosevelt became a rugged guy. He began to imitate fearless men who seemed even a little dangerous. He developed his body and became the New York City police commissioner at a time when that job smelled of risk. He became a judo expert and a Rough Rider. He graduated from Harvard and won the Nobel Prize. He touched all the bases. Why? Because someone believed in him and expected excellence from him.

L stands for *listen.* When a child stops listening to a parent, it's usually because the parent first stopped listening to the child. Parents need to listen to understand. Employees at McDonald's do this all the time. When we place our order, they repeat what they heard: "You ordered a Big Mac, fries, and a Coke—is that correct?" A parent has to do the same thing with a son or a daughter: "This is what I heard you saying; is that right?" When the child agrees, the parent says, "Oh, now I see what you believe"— but doesn't announce what *he* believes. He waits until the child asks. In that way, he values what the child says. And if the parent keeps on valuing what the child says, at some point, the child is going to want to know the parent's opinion. The same goes for significant friendships. I've met many men who tell me their pastors and church leaders don't listen to them. But listening is the first and indispensable step toward forming a significant relationship.

A stands for *authentic.* When we mess up, we need to say, "I'm sorry." Every July 4 our family—me, Lyndi, our four grown children, and our nine grandchildren—spends a week together. Last year, in front of our three daughters-in-law and grandchildren, I washed the feet of my wife and children. I admitted my faults and asked them to forgive me for all the mistakes I've made through the years. Our children wept. I wanted everyone, starting with Lyndi, to know how much I regretted the way I had missed the mark in key areas of their lives. By the end of the day, we had all fallen more deeply in love with one another. Keep in mind, I'm sixty-two years old, and all my children have left our home; the youngest is twenty-nine. As it is in the home, so it is in the church. I believe men yearn for a pastor who will be authentic and who will acknowledge his mistakes.

We can never stop being authentic with our loved ones. When we model authenticity, they'll give it away sooner than we did.

T is for *time.* Kids measure love by time, not by money or by slaps on the back. They know we love them when we sit with them and take an interest in what interests them. If we try to get them to do what we like to do, it doesn't work. But if we spend our time with them doing what *they* like to do, then we have something significant.

E is for *expectation.* Through faith, we expect that God will do something wonderful in the lives of our loved ones. This requires faith, because even if we do everything right, nothing will ultimately succeed unless the Lord does his work. He's the one who makes it happen. Our part is to bathe our relationships in daily prayer, to carry and cover them. If we remain obedient to God, we can legitimately expect that he'll do what only he can do. As the Lord himself says, "Apart from me, you can do nothing" (John 15:5).

When we pay attention to all six facets of the RELATE acrostic, we greatly improve our chances of creating, developing, and deepening the significant relationships that God wants us to enjoy. Yet there are relationships and there are *relationships*. Not all relationships are created equal.

FOUR LEVELS OF RELATIONSHIP

All of us need to develop relationships at each of four distinct levels. While most of us have experience with the first three levels, the fourth level—by far the most important—continues to elude the majority of men in the body of Christ. And it's that omission, I want to suggest, that permits the division in the church to grow continually wider. Most men stop at Level Three, sometimes mistakenly believing that they've reached Level Four. What's the difference? Let's take a look.

Level One: Acquaintance

At Level One, you make someone's acquaintance. You learn the person's name, perhaps a few details about his family or business life, and a few other odds and ends. You say hi when you see him at the mall or in church, but your relationship doesn't go much beyond pleasantries and clichés.

Level Two: Feelings and Growth

At Level Two, you move beyond the acquaintance stage to get to know the individual a little better. Your relationship grows and takes on more depth. You not only add to your bank of information on the person, you also start to experience emotions and feelings regarding your relationship. You genuinely care about what happens to your friend and look forward to seeing him.

Level Three: Confidence and Trust

As you pass Level Two to reach Level Three, you sense real trust developing. You open up a bit more and begin to put real confidence in your relationship. You may even point out this man to others and tell them, "He's my best friend." You spend significant time with him and consider him both loyal and highly valued. You develop genuine trust in your relationship.

Many men's accountability groups reach Level Three but never attain the next level. In fact, many guys don't even know there *is* a fourth level. Too many groups meet for years but never come close to Level Four.

Most of us don't even realize that we're comfortable stopping at Level Three. But we need to reach the fourth level! We need to reach it with God, with our wives, and in our critical relationships.

Level Four: Intimacy

The only way to become all that God wants us to be; the only way to rock our world for Christ; the only way to repair the breach that divides us—is to plunge into the rollicking waters of a Level Four relationship. Intimacy is God's secret place of power.

Our accountability groups lack integrity when they don't pursue Level Four. Why even have an accountability group only to stop at Level Three? The best way to achieve true accountability is to go all the way to intimacy. By *intimacy*, I clearly don't mean anything sexual, but rather total disclosure of our innermost feelings, hurts, and pains.

"Hold on," most guys respond, "I can't go there yet."

Hey, no problem if you haven't yet reached Level Four . . . so long as that's where you're headed. Without such a commitment, however, your accountability group lacks integrity. It comes up short. Gang members build a stronger bond over criminal activity than most of us do over the things of the Lord. Some small groups that began years ago are going still—and still not accomplishing much. The men might enjoy each other's company, but they never reach a level of intimacy. They never become their brother's keeper, never get to know "his other self." They never truly disclose and therefore never really trust.

Unless we head toward Level Four and reach for intimacy, most men of color will never disclose their secret wounds, fears, and hopes. If, on the other hand, we agree to trust each other, to carry each other in our hearts, and to commit to understanding one another, then the man of color may begin to disclose the reality of his life. Before long, we'll begin to stand in his place. When someone makes a hurtful comment, we'll automatically reply, "Wait a minute. Time out! You don't know this guy." And we'll protect him. Once we've felt his pain, we will never be the same.

Only a commitment to Level Four relationships across racial lines will enable the church to heal its wounds. Listen to the authors of *Divided by Faith*: "It appears whites need networks of contacts with blacks, such as in neighborhoods, places of worship, work, and school because this significantly reduces their interracial isolation . . . changes in racial perspectives occur mainly in the context of interracial *networks* rather than by merely having a variety of contacts."[1]

Casual friendships lack the power to change the status quo; only Level Four relationships can accomplish that. Yet in a cross-racial relationship, only the man of color can take the relationship to Level Four. Why? Because he has been to Egypt and returned. He has and still does experience pain solely because of the color of his skin. The majority race wants to get past all of this, but the man of color can't. Virtually each week of his life society reminds him that he is a minority through some insensitive slight, whether bold or subtle. Insensitivities will often occur in your cross-cultural relationship but will not be addressed unless you're moving toward Level Four.

To get to Level Four, we have to put everything on the table. We have to learn from our mistakes and press on toward intimacy. We have to follow the example of John with Jesus. John developed such a close bond with his Lord that it could be said of him, "Now there was leaning on Jesus' bosom one of His disciples, whom Jesus loved" (John 13:23, NKJV).

There is a faith component in Level Four relationships—a faith that depends on God. It takes little faith to believe God *can* do it. But it takes fresh faith to believe God *will* do it.

HOW CAN WE REACH LEVEL FOUR?

While I know of no foolproof ways to reach Level Four, I do know that every Level Four relationship shares certain characteristics in common. Consider the following guidelines:

1. Make sure you're equally yoked

You make a big mistake if you try to create a small group that includes an unbeliever. Only the unwise bring someone who doesn't know the Lord into a group that plans to disclose personal secrets. You must be equally yoked.

Cross-cultural pastoral relationships must not be based on education but experience. The majority culture must approach this relationship by saying, "I'm going to learn. I'm going to grow. I need this relationship." If you believe that the other person needs what you have but you don't need what he has, you will never get to Level Four.

2. Don't take on too many Level Four relationships

Avoid trying to develop too many Level Four relationships. Jesus had twelve disciples, but only three made it to his inner circle—and only one was called "the disciple whom Jesus loved" (John 13:23; 20:2; 21:7; 21:20). A Level Four relationship takes lots of time, and if you try to create too many of them, your attention will be seriously divided. I am suggesting, however, that every pastor needs one Level Four, cross-cultural relationship. The divided church in America needs thousands of these cross-cultural relationships.

3. Your desire must outweigh your fear

A Level Four relationship develops only when you want it more than you fear the pain it might bring. In my experience, one develops intimacy by walking through the room of failure. If you want a relationship with me, but I fail you and yet you still accept me, your commitment will help me walk through the door of intimacy.

Raleigh Washington and I have reached Level Four. To get there we've endured a lot of donnybrooks; it has not been a smooth ride. Both of us have had to repent, probably me more than him. Anyone who's serious about developing a Level Four relationship—especially a relationship with a man from a different ethnic, cultural, or racial background—has to say, "I know I'm going to get hurt along the way, but that's okay. I'm going to learn from it, and so is my friend."

4. You must commit to total, unabridged self-disclosure

Total, unabridged self-disclosure is the only way to reach Level Four. I know of a small group that reached Level Four after several years together. Its members met once a month on Friday evening, shared a meal, and didn't go their separate ways until midafternoon the next day. One man had serious marriage problems and laid it all out for the rest of the guys. Another man began lusting after his secretary and held back none of his struggles. One day a group member said, "My wife has told me, 'No more discussion in your small group about any issues in our marriage.'" Overnight his statement moved the group from intimacy back to Level Three. Level Four requires total, unabridged self-disclosure, yet without descending to gossip or revealing family secrets that ought to stay private.

5. Share your failures as well as your pain

Most of the time we share our wounds and report who has hurt us—but not whom we have hurt or how we have wounded others. Level Four requires that we share our failures as much as our pain. We need to learn in the presence of our brothers to take personal responsibility for our actions and to be willing to explore what may have motivated us to do and say certain hurtful things.

6. Don't judge others

Too often when we've almost reached the level of intimacy, somebody will throw out an accusatory or judgmental statement that shuts down the whole group. We have to come to the table, determined to refrain from judging each other in a spirit of condemnation. If a brother openly sins, of course we are to confront him with his offense, but with the goal of repentance and restoration. As Paul writes, "Brothers, if someone is caught in a sin, you who are spiritual should restore him gently. But watch yourself, or you also may be tempted" (Gal. 6:1). We will pray for one another, we will care for one another, we will encourage and help one another—but we will emphatically refuse to bring condemnation on each other.

7. Make sure no one feels used

Intimacy cannot grow in an environment where someone feels used. If you talk to a person only when you want some help, the man has every right to think, *You want to be my "friend" only because you need something from me.* How do you make sure your friend doesn't feel used? Talk to him just to catch up. Pray for him daily. Call him just to say, "How are you doing?"

Even lobbyists working in Washington, D.C., don't knock

on lawmakers' doors only to say, "Here I am; here's my out-stretched hand." They're trained to make at least seven personal contacts before issuing their requests. If Washington lobbyists focus on relationship, how much more important is it for Christian men who want to build Level Four relationships?

8. Make a commitment to work through the logjams

Every relationship worth having will suffer its share of problems. If you want a Level Four relationship, you have to make a commitment at the outset to work through the logjams. When the water rises and flotsam clogs up the works, you have to be willing to go in and move the impediments so that your relationship can flow freely once more. To change the metaphor, you have to keep getting up and getting back into the game. You have to remain committed to going the distance. When hurt enters a cross-cultural relationship, the tendency is to avoid that arena—but such behavior blocks entrance into Level Four. Get up! Get back in the game!

Mutual submission is the ultimate goal of a Level Four relationship. Keep in mind that submission is not a control word, but a love word. When we submit to those who love us, we submit to their influence, based on the confidence that they desire our very best. And when we reach that level, we really have reached the very top.

A DEATH MUST OCCUR

At least one thing can't be avoided in a Level Four relationship: a death.

An African American friend of mine recently spoke in South Africa to about twelve hundred pastors. He began his remarks like this: "I'm from America, and I'm here looking for the white man who bought me." A howl went up from the audience. He continued: "But I'm also here looking for the black man who sold me."

Another howl. And then the clincher: "But none of that really matters to me anymore. Do you know why? Because I'm a dead man, and dead men don't hold grudges. Dead men aren't overly sensitive. As Paul says in Galatians 2:20, 'I have been crucified with Christ and I no longer live, but Christ lives in me.'"

To get to Level Four, both parties in the relationship have to become dead men. Anything less will prevent them from reaching intimacy. In describing the most important Level Four relationship of all, our Lord said, "If anyone would come after me, he must deny himself and *take up his cross* and follow me" (Matt. 16:24, emphasis added). He meant that a death must occur—namely, our own. So the apostle Paul admitted, "I die every day" (1 Cor. 15:31).

Does all this talk of death sound as if it will take you on an unpleasant path? It's really just the opposite; dying to self takes you into intimacy with the Lord himself.

A man who wants to go to Level Four with his wife has to love her like Christ loved the church—and Jesus died for the church (see Eph. 5:25). Likewise, when you determine to go to Level Four with a friend—especially with someone who's racially or culturally different from you—you must die to yourself. You must intentionally follow the path of Jesus as Paul described it: "For you know the grace of our Lord Jesus Christ, that though he was rich, yet for your sakes he became poor, so that you through his poverty might become rich" (2 Cor. 8:9).

Only with difficulty can we reach the level of intimacy in any relationship, but it may be especially hard for pastors. Many pastors admit that they find achieving intimacy one of their most difficult challenges. Most pastors have no relationship that goes to the level of intimacy, unless they have it with their wives (and many don't). They feel as though they can't afford an intimate relationship with anyone and so further isolate themselves. A mystique regarding the pastorate causes many pastors to protect themselves from the very kind of relationship that they so desperately need. They already feel as though they "die daily"—from criticism over their sermons to complaints regarding their appearance to disapproval of their budget recommendations—so why risk another death by pursuing an intimate friendship?

Let me suggest one reason. While a Level Four friendship requires a death, it also may prevent many more.

A close friend recently took his life at age sixty-five. He had undergone heart surgery to replace a defective valve, and no one told him that a high percentage of patients receiving this treatment experience six to nine months of deep depression. My friend couldn't deal with his slurred speech, slower movements, and weight loss. He felt as though he had become a burden and a liability to his family. Then the enemy attacked, and he committed suicide.

Through this tragedy, the Lord led me to Proverbs 20:5. "The purposes of a man's heart are deep waters," it says, "but a man of understanding draws them out." God showed me that regardless of how deep a guy might sink into depression, a man at Level Four with the Lord can draw out of his depressed friend the things that trouble him most. He can get his friend to say, "I'm suicidal. I feel totally useless." A man of God can help his friend to admit these feelings, pray him through the rough waters, and help him back to health and stability. He can help his friend go where he can't go by himself. Pastors, especially, become effective shepherds when they reach this level with their men.

As the days get darker and as the love of most grows cold (see Matt. 24:12), we will have an increasing number of opportunities to provide others with the basics of life. As we lurch about in a church that's teetering and wobbling, we have the privilege of showing how godly intimacy can heal old wounds.

When we commit ourselves to developing Level Four kind of relationships, we can minister to those sinking in deep waters. We can draw them out, help to save their lives, and restore their homes. The powerful truth here is that intimacy is another way of doing justice.

A COMMON FIRST REACTION

When I talk to men about these issues—when I declare the need for intimate relationships between men of differing ethnicities and explain that many men of color feel wounded and left to die by the side of the road—most hearers automatically defend themselves. They immediately point to their records as evidence that their hearts are right before God. This tends to be the pattern with even the most godly, Christlike people I know.

"Most white evangelicals," say the authors of the landmark book *Divided by Faith*, "fail to recognize the institutionalization of racialization—in economic, political, educational, social, and religious systems. They therefore often think and act as if these problems do not exist. As undetected cancer that remains untreated thrives and destroys, so unrecognized depths of racial division and inequality go largely unaddressed and likewise thrive, divide, and destroy."[2]

When we talk this way to pastors around the country, we often hear a similar response: "But we *do* have concern. We *do* have compassion. We have a benevolence fund . . . we run a food pantry . . . we operate a clothes closet. We know that things might not be right in other places. But so far as we're concerned, our hearts are right." Most of us rush to defend ourselves. And by so doing, we perpetuate a destructive blind spot.

We must come to understand that "racial practices that reproduce racial division in the contemporary United States '(1) are increasingly covert, (2) are embedded in normal operations of institutions, (3) avoid direct racial terminology, and (4) are invisible to most Whites.'"[3]

But we can't defend ourselves and at the same time be part of the solution. When we point to our records and insist that everything's okay, we give a blind spot the power to continue its cruel work. If our records were sufficient, wouldn't the pain have dissipated? But it hasn't. Therefore, we must give up trying to defend ourselves. Instead, we must quiet ourselves, open our ears, and listen.

Messianic Jewish believers have felt shut out of the church for seventeen hundred years! Why don't we know that they feel this way? Because they are so effectively shut out that we are never near enough to them for long enough to hear them. This kind of hurt doesn't get shared easily or quickly. For friends to risk being this vulnerable with each other takes a lot of time, trust, and patience.

When I spoke with one Anglo friend about this issue, he admitted, "Everything within me wants to defend myself. You say that these guys are crying out for justice. I've sat with every one of the guys you mention but one. You've helped me to see that I've never cried with them."

Do you know why my friend has never cried with these men? It's because he's never reached Level Four with any of them. And that's what it takes.

THE ONLY THING THAT WORKS

Relationships are the only things that truly "work" in repairing the division in the church. Events apart from relationships do not work; when the event is over, so are the relationships. And so is the healing.

When Raleigh Washington first came to Promise Keepers, I had a really hard time listening to him. It seemed to me as though he had a chip on his shoulder. It looked as if he had zero tolerance for white guys. But his attitude toward my grandson changed all that.

Derek, my grandson, is half white and half black. Society sees him as black, and the black community rejects him if he behaves culturally white. Raleigh saw the dilemma and, along with his wife, Paulette, "adopted" Derek. In an official ceremony at church, they both promised, "We're going to be Derek's black grandparents. This boy will never get blindsided to find out one day that he's black. We're going to help him feel proud that he's black."

Raleigh and Paulette loved on my family. They didn't judge us; they just loved us. And I began to see in Raleigh a pure heart. I saw a guy battling the racial monster as best as he could. Most of all, I saw a guy whose heart I could trust.

Over many long months we reached Level Four in our friendship. Today I count Raleigh as my closest friend. If I'm in trouble, he's the one I call. If something goes wrong, it's his number that I dial. It doesn't matter when I call, he comes. And I've discovered that I simply can't outgive him.

In Raleigh Washington I have found an extraordinary friend who has been like a father to my own daughter. Through our friendship, Raleigh has been able to share with me what it's like to be a black man in this culture. I find myself anticipating how I can protect him, whether we're in a restaurant or somewhere else. When I see mostly white patrons, I know he's aware of the lack of color in the room. So what do I do? I purposefully get very affectionate with him. I affirm him and let the "audience" know that I believe in him and love him.

Every man, regardless of his color or heritage, is starving for respect and affirmation. Raleigh has helped me to see the tremendous weight that people of color carry every day in this nation.

At last I see how I've been part of the problem whenever I haven't gone to intimacy. But by choosing Level Four, I am beginning to understand how I can become part of the solution.

Do you want to become part of the solution? It's certainly within your reach—but only when you commit to going to Level Four. Intimacy is God's secret place of power. And if his secret doesn't become yours, neither will his power.

chapter nine WINNING
THE WAR TOGETHER

By December 1940 the democracies of the West seemed helpless before a furious Nazi onslaught. In short order, Adolf Hitler's forces had occupied the Rhineland and Austria; annexed Czechoslovakia and Albania; conquered Poland, Denmark, and much of Norway; and removed France from the war. The fearsome Luftwaffe bombed Great Britain from the air while Nazi submarines sank hundreds of thousands of tons of ships in the North Atlantic. Meanwhile, Germany's Japanese ally was flexing its muscles in the Far East, and the Italians had invaded Ethiopia.

The world of 1940 seemed a dark and bitter place, with the very existence of freedom in jeopardy. America had not yet entered the war, and a struggling Great Britain fought alone against powerful Axis enemies.

In that fearful climate, U.S. President Franklin D. Roosevelt delivered a famous speech titled, "The Arsenal of Democracy." On December 29, 1940, the president told his nation, "We must be the great arsenal of democracy. For us this is an emergency as serious as war itself. We must apply ourselves to our task with the same resolution, the same sense of urgency, the same spirit of patriotism and sacrifice as we would show were we at war." Roosevelt rightly saw that America's future security greatly depended on the outcome of England's fight. He realized that only through interdependence could the Axis threat be defeated.

Angry political opponents denounced the president's actions, worrying that he would embroil the country in a fight that didn't concern it. Many voices called for the United States to stay completely out of the hostilities and labeled the war a strictly European affair with little connection to America.

But history proved FDR right; only when the United States began to supply its allies with urgently needed men and materiel did the forces of freedom turn back the armies of oppression and barbarism. By the end of World War II, the factories of America had produced 296,000 aircraft, 531 million tons of aircraft bombs, 8.2 million tons of warships, 86,333 tanks, 12.5 million small arms, and more than 3.8 billion tons of ammunition, from bullets and grenades to heavy artillery rounds. The Free French were armed and equipped almost exclusively by the United States, while substantial portions of the British and Soviet military went to war in American equipment. Without these resources, the war probably could not have been won.

And yet this was no one-way street; America emphatically did *not* win the war on its own. England supplied troops and critical know-how, especially in code breaking and intelligence. The Soviet Union supplied enormous amounts of manpower and kept Germany busy on a second deadly front. The Allies won the war only when all parties—despite some significant differences—worked together.

Imagine that Gentile believers and Messianic Jewish believers drew near to each other in a new encouraging and dynamic relationship. The synergy of this restoration could create an empowering witness across all divisions in the body of Christ. Can you now envision the primary importance of healing this rift before all others? Could it be that, in a similar way, God in his sovereignty has equipped the suburban church to become something like an arsenal for spiritual freedom? God has blessed the suburban church with many of the resources needed to win the war against Satan's forces of oppression and injustice, but it needs the know-how and the manpower of the ethnic church—including the inner city, the barrio, and the Indian reservation—to succeed. Neither part of the church, working alone, can defeat the enemy; but together they can triumph. Only when urban and suburban churches fight together can this battle be won.

NOT THE FIRST TIME

Many times in biblical history God has equipped one part of his family to lend aid and resources to another part. He didn't have to do it this way, of course; he could have supplied all of his children with exactly the same resources. But God loves to encourage interdependence rather than independence within his family. Therefore he habitually equips one member of his kingdom with the proper resources to help another part.

When an evil and powerful "proto-Hitler" named Haman conspired to wipe out the Jewish people in Old Testament times, God raised up a young Hebrew woman named Esther to stand in the gap and prevent the slaughter. Through a remarkable series of events, Esther became queen to the most powerful king in the world. Her cousin, Mordecai, suspected that God had placed her on the throne "for such a time as this" (Esther 4:14).

And why had God so blessed her? So she could stay safe and comfortable in her palace while her kinsmen perished? Mordecai warned his cousin against any such skewed thinking. "Do not think that because you are in the king's house you alone of all the Jews will escape," he said (v. 13). If Esther failed to act, even at the risk of her own life, she and her family would certainly die; but God would raise up some other means to save his people. Yet that was not the Lord's first choice. God really wanted to use Esther to bless the descendants of Abraham.

John Piper, an influential author and pastor, writes, "God does not prosper a man's business so that he can move from a Ford to a Cadillac. God prospers a business so that thousands of unreached peoples can be reached with the gospel. He prospers a business so that 12 percent of the world's population can take a step back from the precipice of starvation."[1] In the same way, God does not prosper a *church* so that it can move from a house of wood to a house of marble. He prospers a church so that thousands of others can be transformed by the power of the gospel, and so that the world can see and take note of the love that Christians in one community have for Christians in another community.

Perhaps the clearest biblical testimony we have of this principle can be found in chapters 8 and 9 of 2 Corinthians. No other passage in the Bible takes such a sustained look at how God intends his children to use the resources entrusted to them.

Paul begins the discussion by describing his practice of collecting money from one church to meet the needs of another. He boasts about the Macedonians, who out of "their extreme poverty" not only "gave as much as they were able," but "urgently pleaded with us for the privilege of sharing in this service to the saints" (8:2, 3, 4). Paul admits that he is telling the Corinthians about the Macedonians' giving to urge them to be generous and to "test the sincerity" of their love (v. 8). And then he says, "Our desire is not that others might be relieved while you are hard pressed, but that there might be equality. At the present time your plenty will supply what they need, so that in turn their plenty will supply what you need. Then there will be equality" (vv. 13-14). Paul clearly implies that the poor Macedonian church had something needed by the church in Jerusalem, and vice versa.

I can't help but wonder: what would happen if the world truly began to see us live out the message of 2 Corinthians 8–9? Most often we speak of John 13:35 in the context of individuals, but does it not apply equally (if not more so) to churches? "By this all men will know that you are my disciples," Jesus said, "if you love one another." Paul seemed to think it did: "Now about brotherly love we do not need to write to you, for you yourselves have been taught by God to love each other. And in fact, you do love *all the brothers throughout Macedonia*. Yet we urge you, brothers, to do so more and more" (1 Thess. 4:9-10, emphasis added).

We live in an age of cynicism and distrust, in a world in which a growing number of individuals reject absolute truth while embracing relativism. They can reject old arguments for the truth of Christianity—but what would happen if they saw the church put love into practical action? They might admire big buildings (from outside and from a distance), but how could they resist an otherworldly demonstration of love from members of one church to another?

A TWO-WAY STREET

Don't miss the fact that the apostle Paul thought of this kind of resource sharing as a two-way street. Twice in two short verses he insists that he wants "equality" (2 Cor. 8:13-14). He doesn't want one church to feel "hard pressed" while the other feels "relieved." This kind of two-way street is critical to creating Level Four relationships.

Our culture presses us to think of "plenty" solely in terms of material resources, but God's Word clearly teaches us to think of people as the greatest resource of all. We must come to understand that we will find richer treasures in relationships than we will ever discover in amassing property or equipment or bigger budgets. Only the riches of relationships can satisfy our deepest needs.

When we consciously partner with other churches, we complete each other. We stretch each other. It's in giving that we receive. The needed resources of the urban church include a rich harvest of the poor, oppressed, and needy, as well as the know-how for effective ministry. Yet the inner city, the barrio, and the reservation have generally not received hands-on ministry by the suburban church.

Churches without many material resources provide us with an opportunity to live out the gospel—and we have that opportunity only here on earth. In heaven we will *never* have the privilege of feeding the hungry, clothing the naked, or wiping away a hot tear, for "God himself will be with them and be their God. He will wipe every tear from their eyes. There will be no more death or mourning or crying or pain, for the old order of things has passed away" (Rev. 21:3-4).

The suburban church needs the urban church if it is to obey God's call to do justice. Dr. Tony Evans, pastor of Oak Cliff Bible Fellowship in Dallas, Texas, and president of The Urban Alternative, writes:

> *Many urban churches . . . have direct access to lower class communities, but are unable to provide permanent solutions to their problems. While these churches are uniquely situated in the midst of the need, they are unable to meet many of the communities' needs . . . because of a lack of financial support, professional training, opportunity, time and sufficient individuals available to mentor others. However, many suburban churches are blessed with financial resources, skilled profes-*

sionals and an available volunteer staff looking for legitimate opportunities to share their gifts and abilities to further the Kingdom of God.[2]

Dr. Evans believes that long-term, life-transforming solutions to the plight of the inner city must be addressed by the church and not by the government. Why? Because "the church, not the government, is . . . closer to the needs of the people. It has the largest potential volunteer force, maintains existing facilities and operates on a faith-based moral frame of reference."

Dr. Evans and The Urban Alternative believe, as we do, that God wants his sons to come together for the purpose of ministering to the poor and oppressed, and to do so without compromising the essentials of the orthodox Christian faith. Dr. Evans envisions partnerships that will "intentionally foster authentic, interracial, cross-cultural, cross-class, and cross-denominational relationships between pastors and churches in urban America and pastors and churches in the suburbs, with the goal of reaching the disadvantaged fatherless in a comprehensive way, as well as in a way that promotes mutual respect for what both groups bring to the table."

Did you hear that? *What both groups bring to the table.* Such ministry is a two-way street. And what could happen if this vision came to fruition? "Authentic, functional reconciliation will occur as churches cross racial, cultural, class and denominational lines to address the problem," Dr. Evans writes. Second, "the church will become the primary answer to welfare, poverty, crime and family stability, providing the most comprehensive social service delivery system in the nation."

Isn't that a vision worth supporting? Isn't that a vision worth pursuing? Isn't it at least worth *trying?*

The suburban church and the urban church have a lot to give each other. Each can help the other to see its blind spots. And by working together, they can show the country and the world what the love of God is able to accomplish.

And remember, the relationship between churches greatly depends upon the relationship between the urban and suburban pastors. The relationship of the churches and their ability to work together effectively falters in the absence of a Level Four relationship between pastors.

WHAT THE URBAN CHURCH HAS TO OFFER

While the urban church lacks many of the material resources available more widely in the suburban church, it has a wealth of other resources critical to ministry success, especially in ministry to the poor and disadvantaged. Consider just a few of them:

1. Outreach experience to the poor

Have you ever considered the first words out of Jesus' mouth after Satan tempted him for forty days in the wilderness? Jesus began his earthly ministry with an inaugural speech that featured the following words: "The Spirit of the Lord is on me, because he has anointed me to preach good news to the poor" (Luke 4:18).

From the very beginning of his ministry, Jesus emphasized his deep concern for the poor. The apostles quickly adopted this concern as their own, and even a "latecomer" and a dedicated evangelist like the apostle Paul could write, "All they asked was that we should continue to remember the poor, the very thing I was eager to do" (Gal. 2:10).

Now, if the poor are going to be reached, who has routinely shown us the way? Who has the expertise to minister to the unique needs of the inner city? Without question, it's the communities of color. The poor live right in their neighborhoods. If anyone thinks they can reach the poor without the guidance and help of the urban church, they're kidding themselves.

The suburban church needs the depth of experience of the

urban church. If it wants to heed God's call to do justice, it needs the urban church's hard-won expertise in ministering to the poor, the oppressed, and the needy.

The urban church can give the suburban church a genuine heart for the poor and the needy. The urban church already has such a heart. It comes out of life experience; it's just natural with them. Because of that, the urban church has a vision for reaching the least, the last, and the lost. Vision comes from passion, and once the suburban church gets exposed to the passion of the urban church, the vision will follow.

The urban church can say to its suburban brothers, "Hey, we can help you to minister to the poor. We have the resiliency, we have the experience, and we have the commission to stay here and stick it through."

2. A fresh way to worship

Pastor Jim Cymbala pastors The Brooklyn Tabernacle in New York City. For more than twenty-five years he has shepherded that congregation from a body of twenty attendees to a church of six thousand members. In the past few years he has authored numerous best-selling books, from *Fresh Wind, Fresh Fire* to his most current title, *The Church God Blesses.* His wife, Carol, directs the Grammy Award–winning church choir.

Pastor Cymbala's church, and many like it around the nation, are showing the suburban church a new and invigorating way of worship. Life in the city has shown these believers many things that their suburban counterparts cannot imagine on their own, and that rich life experience gets incorporated into exuberant, praise-filled worship of a God who delights in his people's passionate expressions of joy.

1. *Urgency in prayer*

Prayer time in the urban church is often based on critical,

complex daily needs: a son lost to a drive-by shooting; insufficient burial funds caused by a lack of insurance; pressing job needs (the inner city has an unemployment rate of about 40 percent); an enormous high school drop-out rate (78 percent); a high number of children born to unwed mothers (60 percent); fatherless children (90 percent); and on it goes. Such pressing needs are everyday experiences for inner city dwellers and create an urgency in prayer among their churches. Prayer is often their only available remedy.

2. *Walking by faith and not by sight*

Because needed resources are often unavailable, urban church members have to walk by faith to survive. While many suburban churches must walk by faith to raise $3 million for a new facility, the members of most urban churches have to walk by faith to believe that their sons will not be recruited by gangs, that their daughters in single-parent homes will not become pregnant, and that their children will stay safe on the walk to and from school. They walk by faith, trusting that they will find jobs, transportation, and medical coverage. Urban church members must learn to walk by faith for daily survival.

3. *Community evangelistic outreach*

Most urban churches have a variety of programs designed to evangelize their communities. The urban church therefore becomes an active and integral participant in the affairs of the community and neighborhood.

4. *Community transformation*

Because the urban church gets heavily involved in the affairs of the community, it often transforms the community through its anti-gang programs, after-school projects, adult education offerings, etc.

5. *A less driven attitude toward life*

May I be honest with you? If I want to kick back and relax, I'd really rather be with my friends of color than with my Anglo buddies. Do you know why? In general, they don't seem nearly so oriented toward project completion and constant achievement as do most of my Anglo friends. I find it easier to relax and loosen up with them.

One of my friends of color told me, "We believe in getting the most out of life and have learned to laugh despite our pain and suffering. If we didn't, we'd soon feel miserable, especially given our historical situation. This isn't a carefree or irresponsible attitude, but it is one you have to cultivate when you don't know where your next meal is coming from."

I can personally testify that whenever I tap into the spirit of fun that so many of my brothers of color embody, I have a good time.

Bottom line? God wants all of his children to exult in the various facets of his nature that diverse cultures bring out. If all human beings are made in the image of God, then shouldn't we get to know God better by becoming more familiar with the various cultures those humans have created? I love the Hispanic community and the humility, mellowness, and sweetness that I find among so many of its members. And I *really* love Latino music! I have learned that the Messianic Jewish community tends to speak forthrightly, with *hutzpah;* it doesn't mince words. Further, when the Asian community gives you a promise, you can take it to the bank. And the Native American community's heart for the family has inspired me on countless occasions.

And so it goes. Everyone brings a unique distinctiveness to the table that enriches all of us. I'm so grateful to God for all of my brothers of color!

WHAT THE SUBURBAN CHURCH HAS TO OFFER

1. Organizational skills

The suburban church tends to attract more business and professional people than does its urban counterpart and therefore has many skill sets urgently needed in the city.

2. Discipleship expertise

For the most part, the suburban church does an effective job of discipling its own. While the urban church focuses on outreach, many suburban churches focus on "inreach." The urban church could make great use of some of this discipleship expertise.

3. Trained missionaries

The suburban church is loaded with missionary-minded people and missionaries. While missionaries continue to be needed in Asia, Africa, Latin America, and around the world, many ethnic leaders say they're also needed in the "'hood."

4. Untapped manpower

God has prospered thousands of guys in suburban churches who haven't yet learned to do ministry. They're "saved and sittin' on it." These men walk out of church every Sunday morning and immediately think about upcoming golf matches. But when they go before the Lord, he'll say, "I'm not interested in how many times you broke 80. I'm more interested in how many times you fed 80." Many of these guys are looking for something real to do with their lives. If they ever get turned on to doing justice, they will feel far closer to the Lord and far more fulfilled.

5. Financial resources

Let's face it: suburban churches have a lot more money than do most urban churches. If God says that his heart beats for the poor; and Jesus says that our hearts follow our treasure; and our treasure isn't going in any substantial amount to the poor—well, you figure it out. Couldn't we in the suburban church begin to provide scholarships for future leaders of the ethnic churches? Couldn't we find ways to partner with ethnic believers to bring the gospel to the city? Dr. Tony Evans of The Urban Alternative has outlined several specific, practical ways that suburban churches can effectively share their wealth with their urban brothers. Why don't we try a few of them?

AVOID UNHEALTHY DEPENDENCY

While I wholeheartedly support and urge suburban churches to work together with their urban counterparts to do justice, I also feel compelled to speak a word of warning.

It's crucial that we learn how to share resources without creating a welfare mentality. Many well-meaning government programs and subsidies have helped to create a poverty mentality in America's urban settings and on Indian reservations. We must avoid those mistakes at all costs.

In the past, I know that some urban churches have viewed their suburban partners as cash cows. But when that happens, we create an unhealthy dependency. We don't want urban churches to say, "Oh, my big brother suburban church is going to look after me. I can relax."

The words of Deswood Tome, a Native American and our administrative director of global ministries at Promise Keepers, ring in my ears:

> *I've seen this destroy tribes and people on reservations. After years and years of federal dollars and missionary support and everything else that comes into an Indian reservation, many of the people have developed a very lax attitude. We don't work; unwise subsidies create idleness.*
>
> *One of the problems on reservations is that people have too*

much time on their hands, and with too much time on their hands, they get into trouble. If they were to use those idle hands to do something meaningful to sustain life in an everyday setting, that would get them turned around. I don't want to create a state of dependency; I want this to be an equal partnership of reciprocating value. That's my caution here.

The best safeguard against an unhealthy dependency is the establishment of a Level Four cross-cultural relationship between pastors. Ministry grows out of a committed, long-term relationship. Sticky issues can best be discussed and resolved within the context of a Level Four friendship. While some unscrupulous urban leaders no doubt have misappropriated funds entrusted to their care by suburban partners, they are definitely the exception and not the rule. Most leaders I know value a solid relationship over a source of revenue.

A short time ago we participated in a pastors' conference in South Africa. Conference leaders had, for the first time, invited representatives from the Zionists, a large Christian denomination. The 4.5 million members of this group are desperately poor and live a hardscrabble life on government land. Most Christian groups in South Africa have effectively ostracized the Zionists; some have considered the denomination a cult. Conference organizers invited a bishop from the Zionists to address the pastors, but he did not say what many expected.

"We are poor and needy," he said, "but we are not here to ask for a handout. We are here to ask for your hand." The bishop's comments reduced many pastors to tears and prompted them to repent of their suspicious attitudes toward their less fortunate brethren.

I think a similar story could be told in the United States. Urban pastors aren't looking for a handout, but for a hand. But for this to work, the relationship has to be a two-way street—because in ministry, one-way roads always lead to dead ends.

THE BARNABAS MODEL

Perhaps we can take a clue about how to successfully share our resources from a Cypriot Levite named Joseph. We know him better as Barnabas.

We first learn of Barnabas in Acts 4, where we discover that he "sold a field he owned and brought the money and put it at the apostles' feet" (v. 37). The money the apostles raised in this fashion they "distributed to anyone as he had need" (v. 35). So Barnabas first served the church by giving his *money*.

Later, after Saul came to Christ and unsuccessfully tried to join forces with the church (he had earned a reputation as a violent persecutor and the believers quite reasonably feared him), Barnabas came along and got Saul plugged in. He vouched for Saul's conversion and his character, and as a result, the church gained a true champion (see Acts 9:26-28). So next Barnabas used his *influence*.

When the apostles heard that the Holy Spirit had descended in power in Antioch, they sent Barnabas to investigate. When he saw the church's need for good teachers, he left for Tarsus to retrieve Saul so that both men might minister together. While the duo remained in Antioch, the Spirit predicted the coming of a worldwide famine. In response, the "disciples, each according to his ability, decided to provide help for the brothers living in Judea. This they did, sending their gift to the elders by Barnabas and Saul" (Acts 11:29-30). So here Barnabas gave liberally of his *time*.

In Acts 13, the Spirit said to the church, "Set apart for me Barnabas and Saul for the work to which I have called them" (v. 2). The pair set off on their first missionary journey and planted churches wherever they went. Before the second missionary journey, Paul (formerly known as Saul) said in effect, "I'm not taking that yellow-backed John Mark. He already abandoned us once when the going got tough, and I refuse to give him a second opportunity to desert." Barnabas argued that they ought to give the young man a second chance, but Paul wouldn't hear of it. So finally Barnabas suggested, "Okay, you take Silas with you, and I'll take John Mark with me" (see Acts 15:36-40). Do you know what happened with John Mark? Tradition says he wrote the Gospel of Mark; and by the end of Paul's life, even the old missionary vouched for the man's usefulness (2 Tim. 4:11). None of this would have happened without Barnabas, whose name means "son of encouragement." First he gave his money, then his influence and his time—but his greatest contribution of all was his gift of love and compassion and respect.

I hope the suburban church can take its cue from Barnabas. Does the urban church need money? Sure. Does it need influence? Yes. Does it need time? Definitely. But more than anything, it needs the sort of love, compassion, and respect that a Barnabas-type suburban church can give.

Remember, everyone in this enterprise brings something valuable to the table. And when we share our resources in a spirit of love and interdependence, both parties come away feeling valued, encouraged, and reenergized.

We can't win this war alone. But together? Together is a different story.

Did you know that the Bible's only direct quote from Barnabas is spoken in tandem with Paul? Acts records many of Paul's speeches, but not one from Barnabas. All we have from him is a single short address that he and Paul spoke together. I think their words provide an excellent end to this chapter:

> This is what the Lord has commanded us: "I have made you a light for the Gentiles, that you may bring salvation to the ends of the earth." (Acts 13:47)

chapter ten GOING FROM GOOD TO GREAT

We used to teach our football players a chant that I think could give us some help in the church. The chant goes like this: "Good, better, best. Never let it rest. Till your good is your better and your better is your best."

God has abundantly blessed his church in America. He has given us thousands of godly, talented pastors—chosen servants who love the Lord, care for his people, and reach out to those who don't yet know him.

He has given us unprecedented opportunities to advance his kingdom and make his name known to an unbelieving culture.

He has entrusted us with untold resources and permitted us to help and challenge his church worldwide.

Yes, we have significant problems, but

in many areas, things seem pretty good. And there lies the danger. Remember the chant? We can't afford to feel satisfied with "good." We must keep pushing for "better" until we reach our "best." Anything less just won't cut it.

Pastors, I believe your men will respond to this kind of an invitation. This is a masculine, in-your-face challenge that will call your men out. This is what a man's man needs. And this is one way to continue "[pressing] toward the mark for the prize of the high call of God in Christ Jesus" (Phil. 3:14, KJV).

REDEEMED BUT RESTLESS

The Bible talks about a peace that "transcends all understanding" (Phil. 4:7). Even in a fallen world where we often have to contend with tragedy and uncertain times, God wants us to experience the soul-satisfying peace that flows from his loving heart.

Yet it's very possible to invite Jesus into your heart, to be a man of prayer and of the Word, and still feel a gnawing restlessness. You can continue to feel a dissatisfaction, an emptiness, a hole that you just can't keep filled. I, too, have felt that restlessness, even though I know the Lord, love him with all my heart, and often go to the secret place with him. Why? I think there's a very good reason.

While it's "good" to be saved, a man longs to be "great." And God declares that greatness comes from moving beyond personal righteousness to doing justice. Greatness comes from seeing a need in others and doing something concrete to meet that need. Jesus put it like this: "But he who is greatest among you shall be your servant" (Matt. 23:11, NKJV).

Do you want to be great? Then be a servant.

211 DEGREES

Place a pot of water on the stove and turn on the burner. Stick a thermometer inside the pan and watch the water's temperature rise. At 211 degrees Fahrenheit, water is very hot. But raise it just one degree, and all of a sudden, something remarkable happens: the water boils.

At 211 degrees—as hot as that is—you can't get a steam engine to budge. You wouldn't want to put your bare hand on its hot metal skin, of course, but the scalding water inside has no power to move the engine, not even by half an inch. But at 212 degrees, that same steam engine can haul a mile-long freight train up and over a rugged mountain pass. It's just one degree. But what a difference that one degree makes!

Do you know why so many guys feel such dissatisfaction with their spiritual lives? They're "hot" at 211 degrees, but they're still not "boiling." It's good, of course, to reach 211 degrees—but if you want to get up and over the mountain pass, you need that one last degree. To go from good to great, you have to move from personal righteousness to doing justice.

The Lord recently pointed me to Jeremiah 9:23-24 to show how guys can move from good to great. In order to truly know God—in order to reach the "great" level—we must come to understand and live by three great truths regarding the heart of God. The Lord tells us, "Let him who boasts boast about this: that he understands and knows me, that I am the Lord, who exercises kindness, justice and righteousness on earth, for in these I delight."

First, God says, "You have to accept my love. You must understand that I am a God who loves unconditionally. I don't love you because of your behavior or performance; I just love you. That's who I am." The only way we can really know God is to accept that he loves us, that he has the capacity and the will to shower us with divine love. This is his unconditional covenant love for those who love him and who by faith in Jesus Christ keep his commandments. That's the fundamental place to begin. In the prophet's words, God "exercises kindness."

Second, we have to be in a right relationship with the Lord. Those who truly accept God's love see their lives transformed by that love. Their spiritual taste buds change, and their craving for the delicacies of sin gives way to a stronger desire for holiness. God says that those who call on his name can't continue to regard iniquity in their hearts. In order to ascend his holy hill and truly know him, they have to come with clean hands and a pure heart. In Jeremiah's terms, God "exercises righteousness."

Third, one who truly knows God has to love his neighbor as himself. And how do you love yourself? You love yourself by feeding yourself, by providing shelter for yourself, by making sure you have sufficient clothes, transportation, spending money—that is, by seeing to your basic needs. The "Good Samaritan" in Jesus' parable saw a wounded man lying on the side of the road and provided him with some medicine, food, shelter, warmth, transportation, and a little spending money—just the basics. In the words of Jeremiah, God delights in "justice."

It's no wonder that so many of us have been missing out on "the peace of God, which passeth all understanding" (Phil. 4:7, KJV), for we've been neglecting this third piece of what it means to know God. It's not enough to invite Jesus into our heart and experience his love and kindness. It's not enough to avoid personal sin and develop habits of personal righteousness. To know God in a way that brings deep peace, we also have to do justice. God delights in all three "pieces" of Jeremiah 9:24, and when any of them goes missing, so does our peace. To experience the deep peace of God, we have to be doing all three pieces simultaneously. That's when God steps in to "guard your hearts and minds in Christ Jesus" (Phil. 4:7).

MOVING FORWARD

God has put us on a journey to a "city with foundations, whose architect and builder is God" (Heb. 11:10). While we remain on this earth, we confess with Abraham that we are "aliens and strangers" and that we are "longing for a better country—a heavenly one" (Heb. 11:13, 16).

Yet even while we live down here, God wants us to behave like those whose "citizenship is in heaven" (Phil. 3:20). That means our behavior has to change, and with it our character, because all of us come into this world with a bent toward sin. God wants our spiritual journey to be characterized by persistent (if not always constant) growth. We needn't fear the blind spots that others see in us but rather ought to use their discoveries as further opportunities for growth.

The Christian life is all about growth. We all have to start somewhere; the trick is to move past the place where we start. If a blind spot has kept us from doing justice in the way that delights God's heart, the wise response is not to deny it or excuse it, but to use the discovery as a launching pad for change. As you consider the following four "phases of competence," which one characterizes your own stage of growth in the area of doing justice?

Phase One: Unconscious Incompetence

All of us begin at this phase. We are incompetent in doing justice, but we don't know it. We suffer from a blind spot that makes our weakness or failing invisible to us. We don't know what we don't know. When someone finally throws a light on this blind spot, however, we can move to Phase Two.

Phase Two: Conscious Incompetence

At Phase Two we're still incompetent—we still don't know how to do justice well—but because a light has finally illuminated our blind spot, we can say, "Wow, I didn't even realize the problem. Now I can take some steps to overcome it." If we have the humility to admit our faults and the desire to surmount them, then we can begin a journey to address our problem. As we grow, we gain further knowledge and experience and eventually move to the next phase.

Phase Three: Conscious Competence

As we exert ourselves to gain the information and the skills we need to grow, we acquire the ability to do justice in a competent way. Most people stop here—but this isn't our ideal destination. The final phase is really "the place to be."

Phase Four: Unconscious Competence

When we work at doing justice until it becomes a part of who we are, we no longer have to stop and think about it in order to accomplish what needs to be done. Doing justice becomes second nature; our actions come naturally, without conscious thought. We become unconsciously competent. A Level Four relationship across racial lines can provide real competence.

All coaches want their athletes to become unconsciously competent on the field. Most players arrive as freshmen at Phase One; they're unconsciously incompetent. So the coaching staff shows them what they're doing wrong and helps them to work out the kinks. Sometimes a coach will take a young man aside and say, "Son, you're thinking too much; just do it." Over the course of his college career, a player discovers more of his blind spots and works hard on them, until finally he becomes unconsciously competent. He does what he needs to do without even thinking about it. His skills become a part of who he is.

Remember Don Shula's vision of perfection? He achieved a staggering level of success because he worked hard to become unconsciously competent. He didn't have to think about what he wanted to see on the field; he knew it instinctively.

God wants the same thing from pastors who will raise up men who are unconsciously competent in doing justice. And

God wants us all to become unconsciously competent in the following areas:

- Grasping and appropriating his unconditional love for us;
- Behaving as a redeemed child of the King who strives for personal righteousness; and
- Reaching out with justice to the poor and needy.

When we do that, our Christian lives start moving forward at a pace we have never known—and we begin to experience the kind of deep peace that the Lord desires for us.

T-R-U-S-T

We at Promise Keepers have been working on an acronym to help us better communicate our desire for pastors and church leaders to do justice and thus enjoy the wonderful peace of God. We define "TRUST" like this: **T**rue **R**eligion is **U**rban and **S**uburban **T**ogether.

If the urban and suburban churches come together to minister to the poor, the oppressed, and the needy, we'll be doing the "true religion" of James 1:27. We'll help one another to identify and overcome our blind spots and will encourage one another along our mutual journey to the "city with foundations."

I know this is far more than a pipe dream, because already we're getting all kinds of reports that men across this great country of ours are living out the acronym TRUST. Godly pastors are leading their men across racial and cultural lines to partner together in the ministry of the gospel. Suburban churches and urban churches are humbling themselves, committing themselves to one another, and working together as equals to meet the needs of the poor, the oppressed, and the needy. Allow me to give you just a few examples of where genuine TRUST is taking place. (And remember, this takes place only where a

Level Four relationship exists between an urban and suburban pastor.)

Denver, Colorado

In our own backyard, we're encouraging predominantly white churches from the suburbs to partner with churches of color from the inner city. We're asking pastors to take four to six weeks to ask their congregations to prepare themselves to go and do justice. At the same time, the urban church is preparing to receive and partner with its suburban brothers. We tell them both, "God blessed you so that you can be a blessing."

It takes time for congregations to get used to the idea that God is calling them to do justice. We're getting copies of every sermon that's preached on the issue, from both sides, so that we can adequately prepare to help. We're also actively monitoring how these partnerships work so we can help address missteps and encourage successes.

Rock Church, Chicago, Illinois

Since Raleigh Washington knows all about Rock Church (as its former pastor), I'll let him describe what has happened (and is happening) there.

> *About one third of my operating budget came from individuals in churches who saw us as a missions church. One of the biggest supporters was an out-of-state church located several hundred miles away. I developed a long-term, committed relationship with the church's missions pastor.*
>
> *Our families became good friends, and he invited me to come to a missions conference, which I did. I challenged them to come to Chicago and be involved in a harvest ministry. They did come, and their visit started what is now a fifteen-year partnership.*

Every year, as part of this partnership, Rock Church and its partner church together put on a week-long evangelistic campaign, complete with tent, gospel music, and an evangelistic luncheon every day. On the final day they feed fried chicken and barbecued ribs to about fifteen hundred people from throughout the neighborhood. The whole thing costs about seventy-five thousand dollars.

When I left Rock Church to come to Promise Keepers six years ago, my friend felt that God was in it. One problem: I left the church at the beginning of a fund-raising campaign to renovate an old theater for use by the church, a $2.5 million project. I was concerned about the timing of my departure. My friend and his church remained committed to the ministry we had started, so he took on responsibility for raising $1 million of the $2.5 million we needed. No one asked him to do that; his action came out of our relationship, which had reached Level Four. We had developed a committed, long-term relationship, and out of such a relationship, ministry flows.

Now, could my friend raise that money from the people of his church? Absolutely. Is it needed in the ghetto on the west side of Chicago? Absolutely. This was an example of urban and suburban working together for the purpose of ministry to the poor, the oppressed, and the needy.

And here's the key: resources and money do not come on the front end. The foundation is a committed, long-term relationship. "Committed" means they're going after the level of intimacy. "Long-term" means this is not a project for a couple of years; rather, this is for the duration. Ministry then grows out of that relationship. That's critical.

Raleigh, North Carolina

Several black and white pastors from Raleigh, North Carolina attended the Promise Keepers pastors' conference in Atlanta,

Georgia, in February 1996. They were deeply impacted by the messages on unity. Upon their return to Raleigh, they committed to respond to the call for unity by forming a coalition of racially mixed pastors. They formed intentional cross-racial relationships between pastors. Today, those relationships remain and have deepened. A number of the relationships are at Level Three moving toward Level Four. On September 11, 2002, a citywide family gathering was called to pray for our nation in the wake of what happened a year earlier. The experience of former similar events suggested that citywide response would be 95 percent white. However, this particular citywide call resulted in ten thousand respondents, of which 25 percent were people of color. Pastor William L. Morgan of Bethlehem Baptist Church said, "The singular reason we have such diversity was due to the 'relationships' we have established and maintained over the years since the PK pastors' conference in Atlanta in 1996."

Heritage Christian Center, Denver, Colorado

Bishop Dennis Leonard pastors the largest church in Denver with over ten thousand attendees. It is also one of the most racially diverse churches in Colorado. Bishop Leonard felt the Lord was compelling him to be intentional in reaching out to the communities of color. When the church had approximately one thousand attendees with few members of color, Bishop Leonard decided to inaugurate a gospel choir. Within a month of this intentional step, 40 percent of the white attendees, including most of the highly capable givers, left the church. Bishop Leonard had a choice to make. He could be selfish and fearful and drop the gospel choir idea, or he could choose to be selfless and fearless in pursuing what he believed to be the will of God. He chose the latter and by the end of the following year, the attendance was three thousand and racially diverse.

Jackson, Michigan

A diverse group of pastors from Jackson, Michigan, came together after the 1996 Promise Keepers pastors' conference in Atlanta. They're still together, not only pulpit swapping, but effectively ministering as a united church to the needs of the poor, the oppressed, and the needy in their community. Tom Ramundo says that when he returned from Atlanta,

> *I wanted to do something, anything, so I tried the first idea that came to mind. With the encouragement of Rev. Walter Harman, an African American pastor in our city whom I had met at the clergy conference, I went to a meeting of the Ministerial Alliance of Southeast Jackson, an organization of African American pastors. I asked if I could join. When they asked why, I told them I was grieved by the racial division that exists in our country and city and just wanted to get to know them better. They welcomed me with open arms.*

Since then, this group has prayed together, labored together, united for services and programs, "laughed together often and sometimes cried," writes Pastor Ramundo. "It has been quite a journey these last half-dozen years. Along the way I've learned much, revised the way I think about a lot of things, and made some wonderful friends among both clergy and laity."

Ottawa, Illinois

Three years ago, racial incidents perpetrated by teenagers caused great tension in this small, predominantly white town in central Illinois. The police chief appealed to the local pastors to assist him in dispelling the negative perception of their town as racist. The pastors united to conduct prayer meetings and a gospel concert, all directed toward bringing the community together.

A couple of years later, Pastor Robert Johnson of Calvary

Baptist Church (the only African American church in the entire county) asked the Ottawa ministerial group to pray for him as he was en route to the bank to secure a $250,000 loan. He needed the funds to repair the old church, which was too small and in deplorable condition. During the prayer time, one of the pastors said, "The Lord is saying that you should not go to the bank. The project belongs to the church of Jesus Christ in Ottawa." The other pastors affirmed this word from the Lord. The project to build a new sanctuary for Pastor Johnson was born.

The pastors, across all denominational lines—Lutheran, Nazarene, Methodist, Southern Baptist, Assembly of God, Christ Community, Evangelical Free, and independent—came together as one. They raised funds, had bake sales, and gave sacrificially. News of this coming together reached the front page of the *Daily Times* in Ottawa as well as the *Chicago Tribune*. The September 7, 2000, *Chicago Tribune*'s front page had two conspicuously opposite headlines: one, "Talk of Peace but Little Action," referring to the Middle East peace talks with President Clinton; the other, "Ottawa Church—A Monument to Hard-Won Racial Good Will." This coverage led to financial gifts from Chicago and from thirty-five states. A member of the Baha'i faith even sent a check, stating that he was compelled to join this unity project.

During the project, one of the participating churches, Christ Community Church, learned that the lease for the building it was using for worship had been terminated. All efforts to renew the lease failed. Although Christ Community Church had been setting aside funds to build a worship facility for themselves, Pastor John Nordstrom related to his congregation that Pastor Johnson's needs took precedence. They contributed to Pastor Johnson's church from their own building fund, purchased a tent, and worshiped therein for six months.

At the one-year anniversary celebration of the new Calvary Baptist Church, the theme was "A God Thing." Ottawa is an example of what can happen when the body of Christ comes together as ONE!

John Perkins, Founder CCDA (Christian Community Development Association) and Mendenhall Ministries

John Perkins, known to many across America as a modern-day prophet for reconciliation, is a picture of selflessness and fearlessness. He founded Voice of Calvary Ministries in Jackson, Mississippi. Long before it was considered wise or safe, John gathered whites and blacks to work side by side at Voice of Calvary Ministries for the cause of Christ. Integration was not active in Jackson. In fact, John was warned by police in Jackson to cease such racially mixed activities. John, in selfless and fearless fashion, persisted in what he believed to be the will of God. He was arrested and brutally beaten while in custody. He lost nearly a third of his stomach and received many other vicious bruises. His response to this brutal beating was, "I believe God is teaching me how to love white folks."

Today the CCDA is the front-runner in bringing urban and suburban churches together for ministry to the poor, oppressed, and needy in America's inner cities. John's annual CCDA conference attracts more than two thousand very racially diverse delegates whose ministries focus on justice issues from a viewpoint of righteousness. Individuals such as Dr. John MacArthur of Grace Community Church; Dr. John Armstrong, president of Reformation & Revival Ministries; and Dr. Gary Oliver of John Brown University all cite participating in Voice of Calvary Ministries as deeply impacting their walk with Christ. John Perkins is the model of how God can use a selfless and fearless leader.

CONTINUING TO MOVE FORWARD

Every day we receive similar reports about the exciting things God is doing through godly leaders from both urban and suburban churches. In places as diverse as Nashville, Tennessee; Modesto, California; and Crater Bay, Oregon, God is moving the hearts of his sons to do justice together.

As the Spirit moves in new ways, men are coming together to transform their communities and reenergize their churches. In every case, they're showing a level of unity in cooperative effort to address the felt needs of the community. They are becoming so effective in addressing the enormous problems that plague their cities that civic officials are now beginning to look to the church for answers to their most pressing problems.

Young people today are looking for relevance. Their favorite saying is, "Keep it real." They're looking for the church to actually help people. They don't have much time for an approach that gives lip service to good works but never seems to do much of anything.

What is happening in these communities could begin to happen all across America. When suburban and urban churches work together—not in dictated or specified ways but in ways they develop together—effective ministry occurs, to the praise and glory of God. And such ministry grows naturally out of committed, long-term relationships.

RESTLESS NO LONGER

God designed the bonds between men to grow resilient and powerful. And it is those bonds of relationship that can take a guy from good to great.

Are you redeemed but restless, as I have been? Have you known the Lord's love and salvation but haven't, perhaps, been doing the justice that delights his heart? Have you reached 211 degrees but still need that final degree to send you boiling and over the mountain pass?

If so, then I invite you to join me and thousands of other pastors and church leaders across this country who are hearing God's call to do justice side by side with their brothers from churches of differing ethnic or cultural communities. If you long for a full experience of God's peace and joy, then join us and serve the Lord by serving the needs of the poor and the needy. In that way, God will move to repair the breach in the church—and we will experience an era of blessing and growth unlike anything the world has ever seen.

May it be so, Lord Jesus. May it be so.

epilogue

■ ■ ■ ■ ■

THE GOOD THING
ABOUT BLIND SPOTS

Blind spots injure. They wound. They cause pain. And they can even kill.

So if blind spots are so bad, then why does God continue to permit them to plague his church? If they cause such terrible damage, why doesn't the Lord supernaturally cause the scales to fall from our eyes?

I can think of at least two good reasons why God doesn't miraculously and sovereignly remove our blind spots. In other words, I see at least two good things about blind spots.

WE NEED GOD

First, our God is a jealous God (see Exod. 20:5; 34:14). That doesn't mean that he is a suspicious deity, deeply distrustful and envious of others. Rather, it means that we were created by and for him, and that when we allow our hearts to be captivated by someone or something other than him, he will do whatever it takes to recapture our hearts.

One commentator, Walter C. Kaiser, Jr., says the Bible uses the word *jealous* to describe three divine traits. Jealousy is:

- the attribute that demands exclusive devotion to God (Deut. 4:24; 5:9; 6:15)
- the attribute that directs anger against all who oppose God (Num. 25:11; Deut. 29:20; Ps. 79:5)
- the attribute that causes God to expend his energy to vindicate his people (2 Kings 19:31; Isa. 9:7; Joel 2:18)[1]

It is the jealousy of God for his people that prompted the apostle Paul to write to the Corinthians, "I am jealous for you with a godly jealousy. I promised you to one husband, to Christ, so that I might present you as a pure virgin to him. But I am afraid that just as Eve was deceived by the serpent's cunning, your minds may somehow be led astray from your sincere and pure devotion to Christ" (2 Cor. 11:2-3).

God made us for relationship and to depend upon him in that relationship; that's why he wants us to bring everything to him in prayer (Phil. 4:6). Problems, especially big ones, force us to seek him (Judg. 2:22-23). Our Lord wants to be a part of every aspect of our lives.

That's one good thing about blind spots. God intends for our blind spots to drive us to him. If we could clearly see everything without depending upon him, we would tend to wander away. Blind spots force us to acknowledge our desperate need for God and prompt us to seek out his face and his counsel.

WE NEED EACH OTHER

Second, blind spots teach us that we need others. Those close to us can see what we cannot see. If we do not want to constantly bump into unseen obstacles and crash into stumbling blocks invisible to our eyes, then we have to rely on others. They see things from a perspective different than ours and can help us to navigate life far more successfully than we could ever manage on our own.

When we recognize the existence of our blind spots and admit that we need others to help us overcome them, a desire to build true community begins to grow in our hearts. Men tend to isolate and protect themselves, but this tendency leads to greater hurt and confusion, not less. To find life as God meant him to have it, a guy has to come out of his corner, leave his isolation, and look for solutions in partnership with others. "A Christian solution," say the authors of *Divided by Faith*, "ought adequately to account for the complex factors that generate and perpetuate the problems, and then faithfully, humbly, carefully, and cooperatively work against them."[2]

Blind spots teach us the need for interdependence and true partnership. Blind spots show us that none of us is an island to ourselves. I need someone to watch my back and you need someone to watch yours. I need others to warn me about approaching dangers and hindrances that I can't see for myself. Without blind spots, I would probably rush through life and miss life itself.

AN ADVENTURE OR A QUEST?

Do you know the difference between an adventure and a quest? In his book *Lamp Unto My Feet*, author Art Toalston said that "on an adventure, you go somewhere and come back again. But on a quest, you go somewhere and possibly never return."[3]

I believe, with all my heart, that it's time for a quest. I am convinced that God has raised us up for such a time as this. He is calling us on a quest to reach out to our estranged brothers and to go together with them where the American church has never gone before. And I don't ever want to return to the way things were.

I don't think God ever wanted Promise Keepers to be a perpetual, million-men-a-year conference ministry. I admit that, for a while, we got so hung up on the excitement of huge gatherings that we would have continued on that track until we died. Either it would have died or we would have died—but somebody would have died. Still, that season of our ministry was a great adventure.

But now God is calling us to a quest, not an adventure. He's calling us to a place we've never been, from a place of no return.

I say, let's get going. And let's go *together*.

about the author

■   ■   ■   ■   ■

Bill McCartney is founder and president of the international men's ministry Promise Keepers and was the voice of the radio program *4th and Goal* from 2000–2002. He has a B.A. in education from the University of Missouri (1962) and is author of *4th and Goal PlayBook* (audio CD) with Jim Weidmann (Promise Keepers/Focus on the Family, 2001); *Sold Out Two-gether* with Lyndi McCartney (Word, 1998); *Sold Out* (Word, 1997); and *From Ashes to Glory* (Thomas Nelson, 1990, 1995). He was a contributing writer to the books *Seven Promises of a Promise Keeper* (Focus on the Family, 1994; Word, 1999); *Go the Distance* (Focus on the Family, 1996); and *What Makes a Man?* (NavPress, 1992).

McCartney is the former head football coach of the University of Colorado. His team won a conational championship in 1990. He has been inducted into the Colorado Sports Hall of Fame (1999) and the Orange Bowl Hall of Fame (1996) and has been honored as UPI Coach of the Year (1990), Big Eight Conference Coach of the Year (1985, 1989, 1990), and National Coach of the Year (1989).

He serves on the boards of directors of the Equip Foundation, Gospel to the Unreached Millions, and Concerts of Prayer International, and he has been honored with personal awards including: Humanitarian of the Year from the Syl Morgan Smith

Colorado Gospel Music Academy (1999); the Evangelist Philip Award from the National Association of United Methodist Evangelists (1997); the Fire-Setters Award from Revival Fire Ministries (1997); Layperson of the Year from the National Association of Evangelicals (1996); ABC News Person of the Week (February 16, 1996); the Chief Award from Chief, Inc., Phoenix, Ariz. (1996); the Spectrum Award from *Sports Spectrum* magazine (1995); and the Impact America Award from Point Loma College (1995).

McCartney lives with his wife, Lyndi, in the Denver area. They have four children and eight grandchildren. The McCartneys attend Faith Bible Chapel in Arvada, Colorado. He enjoys spending time with his family, golfing, and bike riding.

endnotes

■ ■ ■ ■ ■

CHAPTER 1: WE DON'T KNOW WHAT WE DON'T KNOW

1. Anna Kuchment, "The Insidious Spread of a Killer Virus,"
   Newsweek, 20 May 2002, www.msnbc.com/news/751089.asp.
2. Ibid.

CHAPTER 2: THE CORE ISSUE

1. F. F. Bruce, *The Book of the Acts*, The New International Commentary on the New Testament (Grand Rapids, Mich.: Eerdmans,
   1988), 312.

CHAPTER 3: MAKE ROOM IN YOUR HEART

1. Michael O. Emerson and Christian Smith, *Divided by Faith:
   Evangelical Religion and the Problem of Race in America* (New York:
   Oxford University Press, 2000), 130.

CHAPTER 4: GOOD DEFENSE, POOR OFFENSE

1. Edward Gilbreath, "Sunday Colors: Dallas churches continue to
   challenge the racial divide," *Christianity Today*, 21 May 2002, 41.
2. Jack Hayford in a fax to Bill McCartney dated March 11, 2002,
   as a follow-up to a previous telephone conversation.
3. R. Laird Harris, Gleason L. Archer, Jr., and Bruce K. Waltke,
   "Hesed" in *Theological Wordbook of the Old Testament*, vol. 1
   (Chicago: Moody Press, 1980), 306.
4. Gordon R. Lewis, personal e-mail message to Raleigh Washington,
   dated February 15, 2002.

CHAPTER 5: COME NEAR TO ME

1. Emerson and Smith, *Divided by Faith*, 170–171.
2. Ibid., 90.
3. Gilbreath, "Sunday Colors," 41.
4. Aretha Franklin and Ted White, "Think," 1968.

CHAPTER 6: A SHOCKING DISCOVERY

1. *The Random House College Dictionary, Revised Edition*, s.v. "integer" and "integrity."

CHAPTER 7: FOUR OF A KIND BEATS A FULL HOUSE

1. Four of a kind is a hand consisting of four cards of the same value, while a full house consists of three of a kind and a pair.
2. We want to give churches the ground rules for group prayer that we developed. Interested churches should contact the prayer department at Promise Keepers for a video that explains and illustrates how these guidelines can be used effectively.

CHAPTER 8: TAKE ME WHERE I CAN'T TAKE MYSELF

1. Emerson and Smith, *Divided by Faith*, 108, 131.
2. Ibid., 170.
3. Ibid., 9.

CHAPTER 9: WINNING THE WAR TOGETHER

1. John Piper, *Desiring God* (Sisters, Ore.: Multnomah Books, 1996), 169.
2. All of Tony Evans's quotes in this chapter are taken from "Come Near to Me: Reconciling to Reverse the Curse of Fatherlessness," a paper written by Dr. Tony Evans, president of The Urban Alternative, n.d.

EPILOGUE: THE GOOD THING ABOUT BLIND SPOTS

1. Walter C. Kaiser, Jr., *The Expositor's Bible Commentary*, vol. 2, gen. ed. Frank E. Gaebelein (Grand Rapids, Mich.: Zondervan Publishing House, 1990), 423.
2. Emerson and Smith, *Divided by Faith*, 172.
3. Art Toalston, *Lamp Unto My Feet* (San Francisco: Harper San Francisco, 1997).